AF541738

'I had the privilege of meeting Dr Anil Kakodkar. I knew that his leadership and professional achievements were truly remarkable. This book, which confirms this perspective brilliantly, is very much welcome [as it will] inspire the future generation [to] commit [to] the betterment of humankind and the service of their country, as he did so well.'

—Bernard Bigot, DG ITER, and Former General Administrator and High Commissioner, CEA France

'A powerful narration of the life and times of an extraordinary Indian, with whom I have had a privileged friendship and association for over decades. The remarkable feature of this story is [that] it, in a sense, recapitulates and recreates one of the most significant Science and Technology developments in the country since Independence—the Atomic Energy Programme. The insights provided by Anil are very revealing in the context of the complexities and challenges that this programme threw up and the way the successive generations of scientists, over more than six decades, created a world-class institution against all odds—including denials, sanctions and even bringing to bear international regimes, much to our disadvantage. Besides his seminal contributions to India's Atomic Energy Programme, he has been involved on a wider canvas of other national endeavours such as education, rural development, crafting of energy strategies and so on. Further, Anil is deeply rooted in family values and a fine human being. This multidimensional story of a very accomplished Indian is a must for every Indian, to know and to feel proud of.'

—K. Kasturirangan, Former MP and Chairman, Indian Space Research Organisation

'This book, by one of the greatest Indians ever, is inspirational. It reflects the struggles, perseverance and massive achievements in Science and Technology, especially Nuclear Engineering. A must read for all!'

—Tarun Das, Former DG and Chief Mentor, Confederation of Indian Industries

'Dr Kakodkar has been a great visionary, a fantastic planner and policymaker, a statesman par excellence, a charismatic leader and mentor, a hardworking professional and above all, a lovable human being. This autobiography, as per me, is only the tip of the iceberg. A lot more can be written about him, but knowing about his modesty, I am hardly surprised that he has restrained from glorifying himself. I also compliment my friend Dr Suresh Gangotra for very ably giving shape to the narrative.'

—Swapnesh Malhotra, Former Colleague of Dr Anil Kakodkar

FIRE AND FURY

Praise for the book

'Essential read for those interested in India's nuclear programme. A deeply personal memoir by one of India's prominent scientists and civil servants, with valuable advice on the key role of education, science and technology in a globalized, knowledge-based world.'

—Mohamed ElBaradei, Former DG,
International Atomic Energy Agency

'*Fire and Fury: Transforming India's Strategic Identity* is an authentic latter-day narrative of India's emergence as a full-grown nuclear power, written by a person who was at the centre of this transformation. It is a story of a modern-day Ekalavya—the difference being that the author was able to complete what he set out to achieve.'

—M.K. Narayanan,
Former National Security Advisor

'The book by Dr Kakodkar gives a fine account of the major strides in our atomic energy programme, made possible by the contributions of Indian scientists—especially the author himself. It is informative and inspirational.'

—C.N.R. Rao, FRS

FIRE AND FURY

TRANSFORMING INDIA'S STRATEGIC IDENTITY

Anil Kakodkar
Suresh Gangotra

RUPA

Published by
Rupa Publications India Pvt. Ltd 2019
161-B/4, Gulmohar House,
Yusuf Sarai Community Centre,
New Delhi 110049

Sales centres:
Bengaluru Chennai
Hyderabad Kolkata Mumbai

P-ISBN: 978-93-5333-728-5
E-ISBN: 978-93-5333-729-2

Fifth impression 2026

10 9 8 7 6 5

Printed in India

Dedicated to my mother (late) Smt. Kamala Kakodkar,
who was also my first and greatest teacher and mentor.

Contents

Foreword

Our Atomic Energy Programme has evolved in a self-reliant way through the efforts of our scientists and engineers. They have succeeded in realizing a comprehensive national capability in this sensitive area of technology, despite restrictions and embargoes imposed on us through international regimes. While developing nuclear capability in our national interest, we have always maintained responsible behaviour fully consistent with our international agreements.

India has always been a champion of a non-discriminatory and just world order and has not hesitated in stating her position against an international move that violated such a position. We have always stood for non-discriminatory total universal nuclear disarmament.

I have had a long and close association with our Atomic Energy Commission, initially as a member and later as Prime Minister of our country, and have seen the evolution of the programme and the tireless efforts of its leaders at close quarters. Successive leaders of the programme have contributed a great deal in taking it forward and bringing the benefits of atomic energy to our people through its applications in carbon-free base load electricity generation, agriculture, healthcare and many other areas. Several challenges related to technological hurdles and uranium resource limitations had to be overcome in the process. Intertwined with the above has also been the strategic role that atomic energy plays for national security.

While India has always been a very responsible country, it took some time for the international community to recognize the importance of mainstreaming civil nuclear commerce with us, a key factor in dealing with the global threat of climate change. On our part, we had to ensure that our strategic autonomy remains fully protected while enlarging our carbon-free clean energy option through additionality in the form of international civil nuclear cooperation.

I am happy that Dr Kakodkar has penned down his journey on the path of nuclear technology development and the global recognition of India as a responsible country with advanced nuclear technology. He is clearly the key contributor to India's emergence as a full-grown Nuclear Power. I am personally aware of a good part of his efforts in this context. This book, *Fire and Fury: Transforming India's Strategic Identity,* is an excellent perspective on an important era of the history of atomic energy in India, coming from a person who was at the centre of it all. I distinctly remember, even today, a few events of fire and fury that I shared with him.

I think it is also important to recognize that the meaning of our Civil Nuclear Co-operation Agreements with key countries of the world goes far beyond developments in Atomic Energy. Several high technology areas that are crucial as we move forward, as well as our engagement in greater geopolitics, have been very positively impacted.

With India having attained state-of-the-art nuclear technology and the opening of civil nuclear trade; with uranium shortages behind us and vast thorium resource potential beckoning us to address the carbon-free base load energy needs of much of the developing world (including India), specially in the backdrop of global concerns related to climate change, it is time for us to make rapid strides in this area for the good of India as well as the rest of the world.

I am certain readers will find this account interesting and feel proud of what a true son of India has done.

Manmohan Singh

Dr Manmohan Singh
Former Prime Minister of India
4 October 2019

Ekalavya's Report Card

The story of Ekalavya from the Mahabharata has left a deep impression on me. Son of a poor hunter, Ekalavya was keen on learning the skill of archery from Dronacharya, then a renowned teacher in advanced military arts and skills. Ekalavya requested him for admission to his school, meant for children of the royal family. The request was turned down by Dronacharya, ostensibly because of Ekalavya's background. This, however, neither deterred Ekalavya from his aspiration to become the greatest archer nor made him give up on his resolve to make Dronacharya his 'guru'. He erected a symbolic statue of Dronacharya from mud, which he worshipped as his guru while practising and sharpening his archery skills. Over the years, with sincerity and dedication, he became better than Arjuna, who was being groomed by Dronacharya to be the greatest archer. When Dronacharya was informed of this development, he went over to Ekalavya to find out for himself. Ekalavya was filled with joy to see his 'guru' and demonstrated to him what he had learned till then. In keeping with the time-tested tradition of the pupil offering guru dakshina (an expression of gratitude through the presentation of valuable gifts) to the teacher at the time of graduation, Dronacharya, not wishing anybody to be superior to Arjuna in archery, asked Ekalavya for the thumb of his right hand—the most crucial body part for an archer—as his gift. Ekalavya, without a second thought, cut off his thumb and offered it to his guru.

Several people shape each one of us through their guidance and mentoring. Some do it directly, and many indirectly. Our parents, teachers, colleagues, friends, and near and dear ones—all influence us in our evolution as human beings. I firmly believe that whatever we become; we owe to our surroundings. I forever remain grateful to the people who have been around me at different points of time, and the surroundings that I grew up in. I have been fortunate to have come across many well-wishers, who have helped me steer myself at crucial crossroads of my life—sometimes even without being asked for it, and certainly without any expectations. My wife, daughters, sons-in-law and grandchildren, as well as my sister, brother-in-law, nephews, their wives and their children—all members of my close family—are deep parts of my emotional world. They have all tolerated me and facilitated my journey. While all of them are like Dronacharya to me—to the extent that they have helped me, directly or indirectly, to steer myself on my journey so far—none of them had any expectations in return.

After serving in the Department of Atomic Energy (DAE) of the Government of India for over forty-five years, I laid down office in November 2009. I waited for about a decade to pass before I wrote about my journey. Partly because other things took precedence, and partly because I thought allowing some time to elapse would enable a better focus on the important and influential events, keeping trivial things at bay. Around 2017, I began penning down my thoughts, thinking that seventy-five might be a good age at which to narrate what one might want to say about one's life experiences and learnings.

One day, when Suresh Gangotra and I were working on a technical paper, he suggested that I write my memoirs and that he would be happy to help. I shared the initial draft with him. The work that had been lingering in my mind for years and had not been making much progress, primarily because of my heavy and continuing preoccupation with other things that interested me more, suddenly gained momentum. Through several sittings and discussions between the two of us and subsequent follow-up work, Suresh has toiled hard to give shape to this narration. I want to express my deep sense of gratitude to him for driving me to accomplish this task. My wife and my sister have also contributed a chapter each with great enthusiasm and emotional attachment. I feel that has added a special flavour to the book.

Like Ekalavya, I owe a deep sense of gratitude to each of the Dronacharyas in my life. The least I can do is to present this 'report card', of all that I have learnt and done, to them. This book is a humble attempt to that end.

Anil Kakodkar, 2019

CHAPTER 1

The Formative Years

It was the pre-Independence years. My mother, Kamala Kakodkar (née Khadikar), was studying at Mahila Ashram at Wardha in Maharashtra, which was founded by Jamnalal Bajaj, a freedom fighter and a close associate of Mahatma Gandhi. The Ashram was set up to impart holistic education to the daughters of freedom fighters, many of whom had been jailed because of their participation in the freedom struggle.

My mother's maternal uncle, Y.M. Parnerkar, a graduate in Agriculture, was a close associate of Gandhi and was instrumental in getting my mother admitted in the Mahila Ashram. Apart from regular subjects, the lessons included several subjects of national importance, and hands on training in real-life skills such as cleaning, cooking (with emphasis on nutrition), spinning, weaving, dyeing, soap-making, etc. There was also exposure to extracurricular activities, including discourses from prominent political leaders and thinkers of that time.

ROOTS IN HISTORY

My father, Purushottam Kakodkar, had also joined Gandhi's ashram at Sevagram after graduating from Kashi Vishwavidyalaya.

Parnerkar arranged my mother's marriage with my father. After their marriage, my parents got immersed in Sarvodaya activities (a constructive programme for all-round development, particularly in the rural context) as well as the freedom movement, both inspired by Gandhi. They spent some time in Bombay (now Mumbai), where their home became a safe haven for freedom fighters engaged in underground activities. A radio station also operated from their house in support of the freedom movement. I was born in November 1943 at Barwani, Madhya Pradesh (then Madhya Bharat)—the town where my maternal grandparents lived.

My father hailed from Goa, which was then under Portuguese rule. When it became apparent that India would attain freedom, he, along with Ram Manohar Lohia and others, shifted focus and decided to work for the liberation of Goa. He was arrested in 1946, deported to Portugal and imprisoned for nine long years. This was a big blow to my mother. I was barely two-and-a-half years old then. She faced the challenge of survival, livelihood, as well as raising me. Mahila Ashram education, though comprehensive and enriching in all respects, did not have any formal recognition. However, she had also succeeded in completing matriculation from the then Karve University by appearing for the exams as a private student. While this was against the norms of the Ashram and everyone expected her to be punished for violating them, Gandhi, when he came to know about it, quietly put a piece of sweet in her mouth without comment.

MY MOTHER; MY INSPIRATION

Rather than following the beaten track, my mother resolved to pursue training in Montessori education (she even managed to undergo a course run by Madam Maria Montessori herself) and decided to set up a Montessori school in Khargone, a district town close to her parents' hometown in Madhya Pradesh.

During the time my mother was training to become a Montessori teacher, I stayed with my grandparents. I was blissfully unaware of the hardships that she faced. Going by what I heard later from her; she went through a very difficult time. With no financial resources or income, survival itself was at stake. Thankfully, several well-wishers from the families connected with the Sarvodaya and freedom movements, particularly Annasaheb Sahastrabuddhe, solidly helped her in her struggle for a meaningful life. I learnt several life lessons from her reminiscences of those times.

I, on the other hand, enjoyed great affection and care, bestowed by several elderly and eminent people who kept visiting us at Khargone from far-off places—just to check up on us and ensure that we were carrying on reasonably well with our lives.

My mother built the school from scratch under very adverse circumstances. She was new to Khargone and did not know anyone there. It was a Herculean task to convince parents to send their children to school, let alone sending girls to a pre-primary school. Many of them felt that there was no need of a school. I cannot fathom the courage that she must have mustered to build the school in such a situation—a socially important activity far ahead of its time. And that too, when her own survival was a major and difficult challenge for her. The school, Bal Shiksha Niketan, has now blossomed into a big institution.

I was among the first set of students in this Montessori school. Thus, my mother became my first teacher. In fact, to me, she was all three—mother, father and teacher. My school and my home taught me the virtues of self-service, discipline, and being kind to others. If someone shouted or made noise when the occasion demanded silence, no one would shout back at them to keep quiet. Instead, the message would be silently communicated by a waving of the hand or a back-and-forth head movement. There were many educational toys in the school. Learning was fun.

As a mark of respect for our mother's legacy, my sister and I have created an endowment fund in her name at Shreemati Nathibai Damodar Thackersey (SNDT) Women's University. The fund is meant for nucleating and sustaining research and teacher outreach/training programmes in the areas of pre-primary and primary education.

My childhood days at Khargone, although a small town in a backward area with a very traditional outlook and meagre facilities for education, were enriching from a learning perspective. The caring mentorship of my mother, the Montessori school set up by her, the close-knit Maharashtrian community around us and well-meaning teachers—all contributed to a rich learning environment for me.

At the age of five, I was admitted to a Marathi-medium primary school near 'Bal Shiksha Niketan'; Marathi being my mother tongue. Studying here gave me good exposure to the Maharashtrian culture and way of life. My daughters did not have such privilege, even though they studied in Mumbai. In the primary school, I also received the benefit of a double promotion, which saved one academic year for me.

I also spent a significant part of my childhood with my grandparents—either during vacations or earlier when my mother was undergoing training. I still remember several stories narrated by my grandmother from her own life as well as from her mother's life—particularly her encounters with Gandhi. My grandparents have played a major role in mentoring me and have taught me several life skills—'true activity-based learning'.

After I appeared for matriculation examination at Khargone, I moved to Mumbai for higher studies, as my father had been released by then and we had a home there. Khargone did not have avenues for higher education then. Coming to Mumbai did enable me to pursue further education. On the home front, however, the relations between my parents soon became strained. My mother continued to play the role of father to me.

MAKING A MARK IN MUMBAI

The results of the matriculation examination in Madhya Pradesh used to be declared much later in Madhya Pradesh than in Mumbai, Maharashtra. Within a few days of the declaration of results in Mumbai, the admissions to colleges for intermediate courses would be closed. For this reason, I was very worried the year I wanted to seek admission. The results were out in Mumbai, but mine had not yet been declared. Help came from an acquaintance who knew the vice-principal of Ruparel College, Matunga. He put in a word for me to the vice-principal, Professor Bhide, an enlightened educator. Professor Bhide enquired whether I was confident about passing matriculation with first class. I answered that I was sure of that. He agreed to grant me provisional admission and imposed a condition that if I did not pass matriculation with first class, he would expel me. So, on oral assurance, without any marksheet or certificate of any kind in hand, I was admitted to the intermediate science course in Ruparel College, courtesy of Professor Bhide.

Years later, Ruparel College was celebrating its golden jubilee. P.C. Alexander, the governor of Maharashtra and chancellor of the University, was the chief guest. I, too, was invited by the college as a distinguished alumnus. In my address, I narrated this incident of my admission to Ruparel College. Alexander, in his speech, admired the old-time management of the college for the decision well taken, but was quick to add that it was an exception and not the rule to grant admission without certificates. He added, tongue in cheek, that as chancellor of the Mumbai University, he would not approve of such admission procedures.

As mentioned before, my primary school education was in Marathi. But my high-school education was in Hindi—a regional language and also one of the national languages. My education in Ruparel College was in English. I am fortunate in this regard. Often, one hears of debates on the medium of instruction that should be followed in educational institutions. For a country as diverse as India, English has grown deep roots as far as higher education is concerned. The English language has also been adopted as one of our national languages. We need to come to terms with our language dilemma. There is decidedly strong merit in learning in one's mother tongue; but at the same time, in today's globally connected world, the ability to communicate with others in a language that most people understand is of great importance. I therefore support the adoption of one's mother tongue for primary education and a choice of either a regional language or English for higher education, depending on the career a student may want to take up. However, there must be focused efforts to prepare comprehensive educational content in all concerned languages.

I scored high marks in the intermediate science exams at Ruparel College. To express my gratitude, I went to meet Professor Bhide with a pack of sweets. He complimented me for doing well in the exams and enquired about my plans for further education. I was naïve, and replied that I was interested in studying Physics and would like to complete my Bachelor's and then my Master's at Ruparel. He shook his head in disapproval and told me to apply for Victoria Jubilee Technical Institute (VJTI) instead.

I did secure admission in VJTI, and graduated in Mechanical Engineering in 1963.

FINDING MY TRUE CALLING

Soon I had to start earning, as on the domestic front, things had become extremely difficult. My mother was bringing us (me and my younger sister) up with her meagre salary. Her health was deteriorating alarmingly. While in college, I even did sundry jobs like distributing leaflets house to house to earn some money and support my mother. I also worked in the design office of Blanden Cole & Co., a small private company, for a few months before the B.E. results were declared. That was a desperate phase of my life, with tremendous emotional distress. Somehow, I survived.

In those days, the private companies would seek the names of graduating engineers from colleges and write to them directly, offering them jobs. Securing a job was not difficult. I too had my own thick file of such offers. I was searching, enquiring and talking to people who could guide me. Nothing seemed to excite me. Then I learned that there was an opening for a tool room engineer in Premier Automobiles, a company that manufactures passenger cars. I also found out that the expected placement was under the chief tool designer, who was an accomplished engineer. I was enthused. Design has always attracted me. The job looked promising and exciting and I saw prospects of learning something new. So I went for an interview, to be conducted by the department head. While I was waiting in the reception lounge, I saw everyone suddenly stand up on their feet. They stared at me until I stood up as well. In walked Seth Lalchand Hirachand, scion of the Walchand group, which headed Premier Automobiles. I remember him in a white cap, sporting a big moustache and commanding a towering presence. Everyone in the lobby greeted him with folded hands and bowed heads. I too felt compelled to do so.

Nothing personal against the Seth, but it bothered me. The scene at the reception lobby made me uncomfortable. The very thought of performing that ritual on a daily basis put me off. I appeared for the interview, but decided not to go back for the job.

It was around this time that one of our close family friends told me about the Bhabha Atomic Research Center (BARC) (then Atomic Energy Establishment, Trombay) Training School. I did not know much about BARC till then. BARC conducts one year of residential training for scientists and engineers, at the end of which the graduates are absorbed as class-one gazetted officers in the DAE under Government of India. Training consists of regular classes in nuclear science and engineering and associated subjects, along with exposure to a few practical and related aspects of atomic energy. Since the BARC Training School had advertised research and development as the main focus, it seemed to me to be an interesting option that would allow me to work on new problems without having to repeat what had been done earlier. I decided to give it a try.

My classmates at VJTI were, however, not amused. VJTI engineers thought it below their dignity to work for the government. Walk-in interviews were being conducted for some state government jobs at that time. An engineer had to simply go to the relevant government office, announce that he had graduated from VJTI and ask for employment. The office would welcome these fresh engineers with open arms and ask them to start working from the next day. Consequently, fresh VJTI engineers would discourage anyone seeking government jobs. Sure enough, my friends threw away my interview call letter for BARC Training School.

When I managed to recover my letter, I found that I had

missed the date allocated for me—but the saving grace was that the interviews continued over a span of ten days. I reported for my interview at the iconic Express Building in Nariman Point, Bombay, on a date well past my scheduled appointment, and explained to the recruitment officer, P.R. Mer, that though I could not appear on the appointed date, I was ready for the interview. He reprimanded me, telling me bluntly that DAE was looking for class-one gazetted officers and my behaviour was unbecoming of one. I replied that now that I had come, could he arrange for the interview? Otherwise, I would simply leave. He was surprised at my casual manner and lack of desperation. Nevertheless, he consulted the committee members, who agreed to consider me. The interview lasted for about thirty minutes, and I enjoyed every moment of the discussion. I came out with a slip in my hand. It was a referral for a medical examination—which meant that I had cleared the interview. But I was unaware of this. When I showed the slip to Mer, he was surprised that I had been selected, but chose not to let the cat out of the bag. Eventually, I joined the seventh batch of BARC Training School.

I found my wavelength at the training school. One year at the school exposed me comprehensively to all aspects of atomic energy. Tutelage under some of the best brains in their respective disciplines, and the opportunity to interact with eminent scientists of the country in a relaxed atmosphere over dinner, were highly inspiring. Our first interaction with Dr Homi Bhabha was during one such dinner. Several ideas about nuclear reactors, their configurations, their design and other such nuances had already begun floating around in my mind. Dr Bhabha simply outlined the role atomic energy could play in meeting India's energy needs and in its overall development. We asked Dr Bhabha about his wisdom in running a large training school with more than a hundred trainees every year. The programme appeared too small to support that at that time, and many of us were concerned about gainful engagement post the training period. He had visualized the programme growing to a large size. His message to us was crystal clear. Each one of us was free to explore new avenues through research and development. He was willing to support this to any extent. He even threw us a challenge to win a Nobel Prize or an equivalent award. If that happened, he would consider the entire investment in BARC Training School to be worthwhile. He also encouraged some of us to move on to universities and work there, saying that he would be happy and supportive of such migration.

I completed my training with flying colours in August 1964. I was the overall topper among all batches (till then) and disciplines, a record that stood for seven more years.

I was, finally, not only able to overcome anxieties about the survival of my family and me, but was now looking forward to doing something more meaningful. It would be no exaggeration to say that atomic energy transformed my life.

CHAPTER 2

Baptism by Fire

As a topper from BARC Training School, I was sure of placement in BARC in a division of my choice—a tradition that continues to this day. Design being my passion, I had set my eyes on the Reactor Design Section in the Reactor Engineering Division (RED). I was assigned to RED along with four other batchmates from the engineering discipline. We were asked to report to V.N. Meckoni, the head of RED, who also had several other assignments and was a top gun in the Department on matters related to nuclear reactors.

At the time of our joining, DAE was building two units at Tarapur Atomic Power Station (TAPS 1 and 2). They were being constructed by the USA-based General Electric on a turnkey basis under a contract. The objective was primarily to gain experience in the operation of a nuclear power plant in an Indian grid. These were the largest power units to be integrated into the Indian grid at the time and the venture yielded valuable experience. At that time, discussions were being held on the type of nuclear power reactors that would be the mainstay of the Indian nuclear power programme in years to come. Both Meckoni and Dr M.R. Srinivasan (later the

Chairman of the Atomic Energy Commission) were in the thick of these discussions.

When we reported at RED, Meckoni was not in office, and we were asked to meet K.S. Subramaniam (KSS, as he was known to people close to him), who was heading the Engineering Laboratory Section there. Meckoni had entrusted the task of engaging the new officers to KSS till he could find time to meet us himself and assign us to different sections in RED. Accordingly, KSS briefed us for about an hour and explained the organizational structure of RED and the activities of various sections, as well as the job opportunities in each of them. After the briefing, he asked everyone except me about their choice of section. Singled out like this, the top ranker of the Training School was crestfallen.

After all the other officers left, KSS made me an offer. In his section, there was a Stress Analysis Laboratory engaged in developmental work that had some equipment for photo-elasticity studies and strain measurement, and a metallizing gun for metal and ceramic spraying. Nobody was using any of them; he wanted me to take charge of the laboratory. I did not know much about development—or for that matter, stress analysis. KSS impressed upon me that developmental work was fundamental and that design followed only after the former was completed. Such work being an unknown domain to me, I needed to think and so I asked for time to decide. I went home and consulted some people who knew BARC, the developmental work that was being carried out, and the Stress Analysis Laboratory. Almost all of them echoed KSS's sentiments, and also told me that KSS was an excellent mentor and it would be best to work under him. Later I experienced these mentoring abilities first-hand—they were indeed unparalleled. I was convinced of the merits of doing developmental work under the guidance of Subramaniam and accepted his proposal the very next day.

Together we met Meckoni, after which I was formally assigned to the Stress Analysis Laboratory. KSS then led me to the lab and asked me to familiarize myself with the equipment. An officer from fifth batch of the Training School and a tradesman were looking after the Laboratory at that time. It comprised an instrument cluster, a polariscope for stress analysis, strain gauge equipment and an assortment of strain gauges. Then there was the metallizing gun. I asked the tradesman, who knew the most about the place, to educate me. He told me that nothing of any importance was happening in the lab, and that someone had tried to operate the metallizing gun earlier without success; it had been lying unused ever since.

After a preview of the assets of the Laboratory and a brief on its activities, I went back to KSS. The first challenge he threw at me was to get the metallizing gun operational. He explained the utility of the gun, which was to spray ceramic coating for mounting strain gauges that could measure strains at a high temperature. The technique could help in experiments for strain measurements under live conditions at very high temperatures. At first, I thought it was a no big deal to operate a metallizing gun and accepted the challenge. But I soon realized the associated hazards such as accidental fires, explosive backfiring and spraying of extremely hot molten ceramic. The trial of the gun would have to be attempted in a workshop in full gaze of a large number of people, and not in the confines of a laboratory. Generally, workshops have designated areas for welding operations with layout and equipment for carrying out the work safely. I chose this area for the trial but realized that I also needed helping hands. So, I asked KSS for a foreman, a supervisor and a welder. 'No', he replied, 'You have to do it all by yourself.' Once again,

I was put off and my pride was hurt. Imagine a VJTI graduate engineer, a first ranker at the Training School, holding a gun in front of around a hundred mechanics in the workshop, trying to operate it with no extra help! To add insult to injury, he gave me a sermon on Bhabha's philosophy of self-reliance. The fresh engineer could not defy the orders of a superior. Dejected and with my prestige dented, I went down to the workshop, with only the solitary tradesman for assistance.

The scene at the workshop was an onlooker's delight. A motley crowd had gathered to watch the young engineer operate the formidable gun. As the gun was meant to melt and spray ceramic, the blast of flame that it produced was large. If you did not push the gas mixtures in the right proportion, the torch would backfire. To my horror, that is exactly what happened the very first time I tried to ignite it. The nozzle that produced the flame was just six inches away from my hands. There was a big bang, and my hands—along with my whole body—started trembling. I tried again, with the same outcome. The crowd was keenly observing all of this and many more had joined in to watch the fun. I tried again a few times, without success. I then decided to pack up for the day and return the next day to resume the effort. For a moment I thought of going to KSS and accepting my inability to do the job. It was an unnerving experience. But defeat was not in my blood.

I kept trying for a few days, each time analysing and adjusting the gas flows. It was an exercise in learning the whole process all by myself, with no one to teach or guide me—quite like Ekalavya. After several trials, I succeeded in getting the parameters right, operating the gun, and getting the samples coated with ceramic. Promptly, I went to KSS, laid the samples on his table, and said, 'Your coating is done. Here are the samples.' He asked me to take a seat, and said that he had entrusted the task to me because nobody knew how to do it. If he had left it to supervisors or the tradesmen, they would have reported that the gun didn't work.

He was glad that I could make it operational. He then briefed me on my future assignments and chalked out a complete experimental programme on a sheet of paper. He designed the test matrix for me himself. I suddenly found myself in high spirits as I collected the paper from him. As I was leaving, he reminded me of how I had requested him for a foreman, a supervisor, welders, etc. I replied that I no longer needed anyone else. 'This is precisely what I wanted to hear from you,' he said. He had refused to give me additional manpower earlier because had he done that, I would not have tried for myself—and perhaps the gun would not have worked. Now that I had succeeded in doing it myself, I could get some junior staff to operate it. He insisted that I take extra staff. He did not want me to do such routine jobs and wanted me to concentrate on other important activities instead. Word spread about this episode, and I gained considerable respect in the Division.

The metallizing gun could be used for a variety of applications in ceramics. V.K. Murthy was head of the Ceramics Section, which was adjacent to our Engineering Hall. Murthy and KSS were good friends, and many jobs related to ceramic coating started coming to us. I recollect two of them. One was from the Department of Space. The graphite nozzles they were using for the Centaure sounding rockets, which were being fired from Thumba[1], needed ceramic coating. The other was from the Ordnance Factory, Khamaria. They were manufacturing shoulder-fired missiles with small-diameter metallic nozzles that also needed ceramic coating. While we were doing such jobs for other organizations, Pereira, a

[1]A place near Thiruvananthapuram, which hosts India's first spaceport for launching sounding rockets

welding foreman, cautioned me, 'Sir, you be careful. Else you will be doing only this throughout your life.' But Subramaniam had other plans for me. We did many coatings for the Department of Space and the Ordnance Factory. Eventually, they set up their own facilities and we went back to concentrating on our work.

Ceramic coating was a messy job. The spray often diverged and the sparks would fly all over the place. In the morning I would set out for work donning a neat pair of trousers, and when I returned home in the evening, they would be full of holes—resembling a sieve. My mother got curious. When I told her the reason, she reprimanded me, saying, 'Dangerous fellow, what are you up to?' But I was enjoying my work, because it established tremendous credibility and respect for me in the office.

FOREIGN SHORES

We continued doing experiments on stress analysis, although nothing of much significance. Meanwhile, planes loaded with engineers started leaving on deputation to Canada. The collaboration between the two countries to build Pressurized Heavy Water Reactors (PHWRs) had commenced and was in full swing, and this had created several opportunities for training. My turn for deputation came within a year of joining BARC. By that time, I had developed a friendship with S.N. Seshadari, who was a top-notch graduate of the second batch of the BARC Training School. He told me that he had been deputed to Massachusetts Institute of Technology (MIT), USA, to do his Master's degree. I requested KSS that I should also get an opportunity to go abroad for higher studies, which I had an unfulfilled desire for. Moreover, I thought that university learning would prepare me for better roles in the future as opposed to training, which, while well-aligned and hands-on as far as the immediate programme was concerned, could be too narrowly focused. Subramaniam explained that while this had been a practice earlier, things had changed. Presently, the policy was not to send officers for higher studies abroad.

This was not convincing. I stood firm. Subramaniam then tried to stress that if I declined deputation, then some junior would have to be given a chance, and I would be left behind. I replied that it didn't bother me, but I would go only if it was for higher education at a university. The matter escalated and Meckoni summoned me. I stood by my request. He too was firm and said that the Department was not running a charity and I should abide by the instructions. I was not at all convinced, and was ready to lose the opportunity to go abroad if such was the case.

I was also mindful of my family obligations—primarily, taking care of my mother and my sister. My mother's health had been continuously deteriorating. She had to undergo a major surgery, which was followed by a prolonged and serious illness. With nobody to take care of her at home, my sister had to be left at a day care. Me getting a job in BARC had brought significant relief to the family, and I could not allow the situation to deteriorate again. My desire to study further had therefore always been constrained by family obligations being my priority. The possibility of going abroad on deputation for higher studies, as had happened for other officers, thus appeared to me an attractive proposition and a justifiable demand.

My stubbornness meant that many officers junior to me went abroad for training before me. Out of frustration, I started applying for jobs outside and attending interviews. KSS, who was watching me all along, suggested that I apply for a commonwealth fellowship. He tried very hard to support me, but nothing seemed to be working. Ultimately, KSS cleverly succeeded in getting an

International Atomic Energy Agency (IAEA) fellowship for me, even though we had stopped availing the fellowship due to issues related to the Non-Proliferation Treaty (NPT). It allowed me to go to the University of Nottingham for an MSc programme. Interestingly, Nottingham was chosen because it was the only university offering a masters course in experimental stress analysis, the area of my primary work during that time.

I landed in Nottingham in September of 1968 for a one-year course. After I got my admission, the floodgates opened and many engineers subsequently went abroad for further studies on various fellowships. Once again, I realized the power and importance of a mentor. I had only expressed my well-determined wish. Subramaniam honoured my wish, steered me through the procedures, and found a way for me to get what I wanted when the departmental policy did not provide for such opportunities.

By the end of July 1969, I had finished my examinations, submitted my thesis, and was waiting for my viva voce examination. I requested Professor H. Fessler to conduct my viva voce at the earliest, so that I could go back to India. He asked me why I was so impatient, since the tenure of my fellowship lasted till September, and requested me to stay back for good. I refused, because I was clear about where my priorities and loyalties rested. He then made me another offer—if by the age of twenty-eight I did not rise to the level of a professor, I could come back to Nottingham University and he would appoint me a professor, even if I did not have a PhD. I politely declined, saying that such a situation would never arise. Professor Fessler also helped me in another way. During the Christmas vacation, he arranged for me to visit various laboratories in the UK where I witnessed, first-hand, large-scale stress analysis work involving big components. I saw component integrity experiments, testing of large components, stress analysis of internal combustion engines, aircraft engines, railway engines, structures, piping and a lot more. Observing stress analysis work being carried out on real-life components in the major laboratories was a rich experience.

One year in the UK also gave me an opportunity to witness British culture at close quarters. The experience was very different from the perception I had of the British, judging from their presence in India. The administrative systems in the UK were based on trust, whereas what they had set up back in India was based on distrust. And while one could sense racial prejudice while in the city, the atmosphere in the University was far more open and liberal.

However, my endeavour to enrol for higher studies in universities abroad led to several other interesting developments. KSS, in fact, suggested that I could register for PhD at a university in India itself. This was a common practice in BARC, but restricted to disciplines of basic science; there were no guides in engineering at BARC at that time. There was a perception that working for higher qualifications based on the research one was already engaged in was acceptable for scientists, but not for engineers. The latter were expected to run facilities, build projects and also develop products and processes needed for the programme, but they were not encouraged to pursue research that enabled them to acquire higher qualifications. I tried hard to work around this by exploring several possibilities. The systems, however, were so rigid that nothing seemed to work. I enquired in some universities, but there were no provisions for registration as an external student.

I went to Professor Sukhatme at the Indian Institute of Technology (IIT), Bombay. He asked me to join IIT full-time to pursue a PhD, but I was reluctant to interrupt my work at BARC for the two to three years it would take me to complete a doctoral study. In any case, my family responsibilities would not have allowed me to take leave without pay for this purpose. He then came up with a brilliant idea: 'Why don't you create a large enough experimental facility, which probably cannot be built in IIT, for your doctoral research in BARC itself? Think of a topic that is of interest to both IIT and BARC. It will be a fit case to argue for external registration.' The proposition appealed to me, and with KSS's support, I decided to work on the heat transfer problem—a core area of expertise for Prof. Sukhatme—although I was well on course to pursue experimental stress analysis.

I decided to work on experimental reactor thermal hydraulics that would need a large experimental loop. KSS was generous and offered equipment and material not in use otherwise. A key piece of equipment was a canned motor pump that had to be repaired before being put to use. The facility was built by me using in-house resources, without having to buy anything specifically for this work. I got a lot of help and support from H. Ramamoorthy in this endeavour. Together, we assembled the experimental set up.

The day before the first trial, I spent a sleepless night, anxious about its success. I must say that this was the last time in my life that I had disturbed sleep; never again did I have difficulty in getting sound sleep at night. The demands on the parameters and control were extremely tight, and I was not sure how the system would respond. But the trial was successful, and I was ready with my research facility for doctoral studies. Just then, my deputation to the UK for MSc came through, and my career took a turn. But the efforts did not go to waste, as the loop was used for research and continued to be in operation for several years.

These events have left a deep impact on me. Comprehensive research covering all aspects, ranging from basic research all the way up to full-scale qualification of technology and equipment, is a must in order to realize self-reliance in nuclear technology.

Treating scientists and engineers differently is counterproductive for this purpose. Perhaps it is a result of the disconnect that manifested out of the 'silo' mentality that has deep roots in our society. We need to be able to seamlessly translate an idea into its practical deployment, and that needs collaboration among people with diverse expertise and capabilities. I am glad that today the situation, both within BARC and in universities, has improved.

When I returned to India after completing my MSc, there were a host of assignments waiting for me. Designing a Pulsed Fast Reactor and validating the structure and the energy management system of the newly evolved containment design of Madras Atomic Power Project were two prominent ones, besides many others. An ever-increasing number of assignments kept pouring in—all with steep schedules. Engagement with different projects of the atomic energy programme started getting intense. My group also started growing. My professional life changed completely.

Having accomplished the keenly desired university studies abroad, it was time for me to focus on the much-needed hardcore engineering development work. It was indeed a massive challenge to develop a programme that would enable self-reliant capabilities in PHWR, a mainstay of the Indian nuclear power programme.

The subsequent turn of events and my deep and purposeful engagement with the atomic energy mission became so intense, that my desire to acquire further educational qualifications took a back seat—never to come to the forefront again.

CHAPTER 3

Dhruva—The Birth of a Star

By the '70s, development of the PHWR programme had gained momentum following the decision to build two more units at Narora, in the state of Uttar Pradesh. The site falls in the Indo-Gangetic alluvial plain and is seismically more active than the earlier two sites, namely Rawatbhata near Kota and Kalpakkam near Chennai. Therefore the reactor structure required a major change. It was decided to model the reactor's structural configuration in a manner that would also be consistent with the larger-sized reactor that might be necessary in the future. A great number of developmental problems were identified. I, along with my colleagues, got working on these challenges.

One day, I received a call from Meckoni, who by then had become Director of our Group. The Group, alongside the R&D work for the PHWRs that was ongoing, was also busy designing a new research reactor, code named R-5. G.G. Joshi, an engineer from the first batch of the Training School, had been in-charge of the pile block (the terminology then used for the main reactor block of R-5). Meckoni had called to inform that Joshi had resigned, and wanted me to step into his shoes. This came as a bolt from the blue.

I had been hearing tales of squabbles between various groups involved in the design of R-5. The major debate was over the choice of system configuration to be adopted. The engineers from the division designated for operations were in favour of a full tank system, which had been used in the National Research Universal (NRU) Reactor in Canada—on which they wanted to model R-5. The designers from engineering and controls divisions were keen on level control, which was a new concept with additional advantages. Those in favour of the full tank concept argued that it was time-tested in NRU and deviating from that concept would be venturing into unknown territory. The engineers involved in this debate were my seniors—some from the first/second batch of the Training School, and most even more senior than that. I had been hearing about this debate as an outsider, and was doubtful of the conviction of some members of the design team. They believed that the reactor would never be built, though the message from the top-level management—to build the reactor—was loud and clear.

I told Meckoni, 'I am a small fry and if I get in, these big fellows will chew me out.' Meckoni insisted that I should not worry about them. The Department was serious about building the reactor and all relevant decisions would be taken at higher levels by someone else. I then insisted that I should have the freedom of developing my own concept and would not be bound by the earlier designs. Surprisingly, Meckoni had no objection to that. So I agreed, but with a rider—I asked him for an 'abhaydaan', a kind of safe passage. Meckoni was stuck in a precarious situation, as he was also the overall in-charge of the project. I assured him that I would put in my sincere efforts to make sure that everything was perfect, but to err is human. In case I made a mistake, he should protect me from the sharks. Meckoni didn't promise me that explicitly, but conveyed enough through gestures to indicate that I need not worry. I took up the challenge. The orders were immediately issued and I got the charge of designing the heart of the reactor.

THE R-5 CHALLENGE

The very next day, Meckoni summoned me to explore the possibility of procuring the complete stock of stainless steel plates required for building the reactor. At that time, the Fast Breeder Test Reactor (FBTR) project was being executed at Kalpakkam, about 80 km from Madras. A.P.S. Krishnan, a senior officer from the Directorate for Purchase and Stores, had informed Meckoni about the funds available for FBTR procurement, which were about to lapse with the financial year ending on 31 March 1973. He had also informed Meckoni that there was sufficient stock of plates available with a company in France, and that he could complete the necessary procurement formalities and order the material if a clearance was given. All that he required from us was purchase indents with relevant specifications. Meckoni asked me if I could prepare the indents.

We were already in March. I had just assumed charge and was not sure how things would work out. Meckoni had confidence in me and asked me to figure something out. I insisted that I would need to finalize the broader concept and prepare general arrangement drawings, if not detailed one. Such drawings would require formal approval before an indent for materials could be raised. Meckoni was known to be a careful officer, and wouldn't sign on the drawings easily. To my surprise, he assured me that approval of the drawings would be prompt. With a team of about ten young engineers, including M.K. Nema, M.M. Singh, H.P. Vyas, R.K. Sinha and few others, I got down to work.

As soon as I began my new assignment, several seniors, who had all been in the project for several years, descended. They interrogated me about my reasons for accepting the task. They insisted that the reactor would never be built and that I, as a young and budding engineer, was wasting my time. I was angered by their callous attitudes. They had been working on the project for more than four years; they had been debating and conducting meetings without any belief in their hearts that the reactor would see the light of the day. I bluntly told them that if they did not have the conviction that the reactor would be built, then they should say so in a formal meeting. I was clear in my mind about the national requirement to build a new research reactor, as the other research reactor, CIRUS, was getting old. There would soon be a need for a new reactor. The requirement of a new research reactor was also linked to the strategic programme, making it important for national security.

Meanwhile, I had the immediate task of preparing the drawings. I worked day and night to prepare drawings that would stand the test of time. Those days, there were no computers and drawings had to be made by hand, using T-squares and set squares on a drawing board. Meckoni and I would hold extensive discussions on design aspects. We regularly met in his office for a couple of hours every day. The intense discussions with Meckoni and the hard work being done by my group were leading to clarity in concept development and shaping the general arrangement of the reactor.

Then, one day, Meckoni brought in another twist. On the debate about the two concepts—full tank versus level control—he wanted the decision to emerge naturally, being the head of both groups. My design of the structure was not to become the deciding factor in favour of either of the two concepts. It had to be such that it could accommodate either of them. Being the seniormost on both sides, he could have easily imposed a decision, but he wanted the two sides to argue it out and arrive at a consensus. I told him that to design a pile block that could accommodate either concept was a tall order, but I would try my best.

The core of a nuclear reactor has fuel channels arranged in a particular geometry. NRU had its fuel channel designed in a hexagonal pitch. Accordingly, R-5 was also being designed to have a hexagonal pitch. I told Meckoni that if he wanted to have the reactor designed to accommodate both concepts, then it would be necessary to take water from each channel out through individual tail pipes—and that would not be possible with a hexagonal pitch. I would have to switch to a square pitch. He was quick to reply, 'Then change pitch to square.' I knew that the arrangement of pitch had strong reactor physics connotations, and that was within another domain, for which the responsibility was entrusted to someone else. I could not take a unilateral decision on the issue. Meckoni held the view that although the volume distribution between fuel and moderator was a physics issue, the geometry of pitch, whether hexagonal or square, was an engineering matter and I could take a decision on my own, independent of the reactor physics group. In a way, he was right. He told me to make an alternate square pitch design without affecting the volumetric proportion between fuel and moderator. That cleared the way. I then made about a dozen general arrangement drawings based on the square pitch. I was racing against another deadline.

I had to raise indents based on the drawings before 31 March, which was fast approaching. I could do so only after the drawings were approved. When I reminded Meckoni, he promptly asked me to bring the drawings—and he immediately approved them and decided to sign! But that was not enough. The drawings also had to be approved by all groups that were concerned or were interfacing with the pile block. When I pointed this out to him, he said he was approving the drawings in his capacity as my immediate superior. The other group leaders were free to do an independent review and make their comments as they wished. He would deal with them if the need arose—in his capacity as *their* superior.

This seemed rather tricky. Nevertheless, I sent the drawings to other group leaders for their approval, with Meckoni's signature already on them. First, I approached Seshadari, who was in-charge of controls—a key element of a reactor. Seshadari was a good friend and immediately signed wherever I asked him to sign. I did tell him that he may find difficulty in accommodating his control systems. He put the ball back in my court: 'No problem; I will ask you only to solve that for me.' Such was the mutual confidence between us.

The next big obstacle was to obtain clearance from the reactor physics group. Convincing Sundaram, Veeraraghavan and Ranganatha Rao was a formidable challenge. I had sent the drawings to them and they had spent hours debating the design. After they had studied it sufficiently, they summoned me. They asked me how I dared to change the pitch from hexagonal to square. I feigned ignorance and said, 'I have not altered the physics core.' I requested them to run a calculation before commenting on the drawings. They could then make whatever observations they might have on the design. Upon running their calculations, they were surprised to arrive at numbers very similar to their original design. Regardless, they continued to question me about the reasons behind changing the core geometry. Finally, seeing that Meckoni had already signed, Veeraraghavan cleared the drawings, albeit with some reservations. We finalized them, raised the indents and placed the order for procurement before the month drew to a close. Within two months, we had all the stainless steel plates needed for the reactor, out of the budget allocated for FBTR.

This was also the time when I faced intimidation of a strange kind. One day, I was waiting in the lobby of the CIRUS reactor. In walked Ranganath Rao, the head of reactor operations. On seeing me, he thundered in front of all those present, 'If ever you build that reactor, I will hoist you on top of the CIRUS dome and hang you.' They simply did not want anything other than known configurations, and were scared of such first-of-their-kind innovations. They had grown complacent with CIRUS, which is a replica of the National Research Experimental (NRX) reactor of Canada. The bigger reactor, NRU, was the natural choice to imitate for the R-5.

The full tank versus level control debate was as yet unresolved. Seshadari was inclined towards level control. He asked my opinion. I, too, was in favour of level control, but I explained that my design was capable of accommodating either of the two concepts. Seshadari said he was planning to meet Dr A.K. Ganguly, the chief of safety and a member of the implementation committee for the new reactor. Seshadari and I thought that if we could convince Dr Ganguly and get his support, we could get a decision in our favour. Dr Ganguly was an experienced scientist with deep insights into safety. He was very perceptive and had a strong sixth sense. We met him and made a presentation. Details of both systems were explained to him. All the merits of level control were highlighted. After about an hour of presentation, he, with a jovial face, announced, 'You have made a wonderful presentation. I have understood nothing.' We then pleaded with him to back us in the implementation committee. He asked us how confident we were about level control, and we both said, '100 per cent.' Dr Ganguly consented,

'I am with you.' That clinched the issue. Formal meetings followed and level control was adopted.

There were, of course, more hurdles to clear.

GETTING ALL STAKEHOLDERS ON BOARD

Now that the issue of level control had been settled, the next big challenge was to design replaceable guide tubes and get the design accepted by all stakeholders. Normally the channels in a reactor core are attached at both the ends. Since R-5 was being designed as an experimental reactor, I wanted it to be designed so that it had maximum flexibility to facilitate a variety of experimental trials (somewhat like a Meccano set). The idea was that the guide tubes would be replaceable. But to allow the tubes to be pulled out, a detachable joint was required at the bottom that would separate coolant and moderator water with minimum cross leakage. It had to be located at one end of a 30-feet-long vertical assembly. It was difficult to make it 100 per cent leak proof, but it could be engineered to be sufficiently leak-tight. Special metallic seals were devised. We were confident that although the system may leak a bit, it would provide functional operability without any compromise on safety.

My detractors were once again nervous. Their concern was about the unintended level change that, in their opinion, could take place inside the calandria[2] with serious safety consequences. They were also concerned about the pressure surge created on the starting or stopping of a coolant pump leading to the fluctuation of the level in the calandria. I tried explaining that nothing of that kind would happen. The level would stay put. It was a simple

[2]Calandria of a nuclear reactor is the main vessel containing reactor internals, fuel, coolant and other critical components.

principle, based on Bernoulli's theorem. But no matter how much I argued with them, they would not be convinced. Ultimately, I decided to demonstrate through an actual experiment. I built a scaled-down model in the engineering hall. I showed the system working without any meaningful seal at the bottom of the guide tube. This was to simulate a non-functional seal. After the demonstration of a stable level under a variety of perturbations, they had no resistance left—but I suspect that deep down in their hearts, they were not convinced.

The hurdles in the R-5 project were far from over. I had decided to adopt electron beam welding for the calandria lattice positions—a process that would be considered highly advanced even today. There were several advantages to this choice. This possibility came to my mind as my Training School friend, Anil Thakur, was developing an electron beam welding machine that could weld such large structures on the shop floor. To my knowledge, there was only one such electron beam-welded large vessel before R-5. The work was completed in the BARC central workshop using an imported electron beam welding machine that was custom-designed to our specifications. The R-5 calandria also has the distinction of adopting some of the largest neutron beam holes, made of electron beam-welded zircaloy cans, as well as some of the largest and thinnest dissimilar metal joints, made by a mechanical rolling process.

During a review, an issue related to creating some additional pressure margin in the design of the calandria was raised. Since the design was finely balanced, taking into account the needs of process, structural design, electron beam welding and construction materials, a change in the pressure rating was neither called for nor feasible. I therefore opposed the change. The matter escalated to higher and higher levels and finally reached the Chairman, Dr Homi Sethna. He was furious at me for my defiance of several of my seniors. I was made to appear before him to defend the position that I was so adamant about. Despite a fiery start, I managed to convince him of the merit of my design and the fallacy in the logic that was being projected to him. He even apologized for having wasted my time as well as his own, and became very friendly and supportive of all my endeavours thereafter.

The 100 MW research reactor R-5 went critical on 8 August 1985.[3] It was given its name, Dhruva (meaning the Pole Star), in 1983 by the then president Giani Zail Singh during his visit to BARC.

However, hurdles still continued for Dhruva. The reactor was plagued with a persistent vibration problem. The problem was overcome following a systematic approach involving diagnostics, analysis and design modification. While this was happening, the atmosphere was tense. A story had started doing the rounds that Dhruva would never be operable.

The reactor has been working fine for more than three decades now and has supported some of the finest and most critical experimental work, apart from the important strategic purpose (national security) it serves. But perhaps it is time to make another Dhruva in the country now.

PASSION FOR DESIGN

When I returned from the UK after completing my MSc, a number of projects were waiting for me. One of them was the pulse fast reactor, being piloted by Dr Iyengar. The pulsing of the reactor was to be achieved by sweeping a block of reflector mounted on the tip of a high-speed rotor past a fast reactor

---

[3]Going 'critical' in nuclear parlance is the starting of a nuclear reactor.

core consisting of plutonium. That would lead to a pulse in core reactivity, taking the reactor to very high flux level for a short time. My task was to design the reactor—particularly the rotating reflector assembly—to start with. The reflector block was to be made of beryllium and the rotor assembly was to be 2 metres in diameter, designed to rotate at a speed of 3000 revolutions per minute. I told Dr Iyengar that it was important to test the assembly for endurance before using it in the actual reactor. We decided to do the testing in a pit under a shed in the open, where it would be safe. This required the permission of the architect, R.B.J. Patel. He rejected the proposal outright, saying that it did not fit into the 'grammar' of the surroundings. I did not really understand what that meant, but BARC has some of the best landscaping anywhere in the world and perhaps the aesthetic beauty of the Centre would be marred. I left it to Dr Iyengar to resolve the issue, but then the priorities changed. There was a mandate to carry out a Peaceful Nuclear Explosion (PNE). The plutonium found a better use and the pulse fast reactor had, literally, a quiet burial.

Apart from Dhruva, as mentioned earlier, I was also working on the development of components and systems for PHWRs. Persistent problems were being encountered with the end shield of unit one of the Rajasthan Atomic Power Station (RAPS 1).[4] RAPS 1 had been a flagship of the PHWR programme, since it was the first such reactor built in India. Reliable and sustained reactor operation was being hampered. The key issue was radiation embrittlement of the end shield material leading to frequent cracking of tube sheet ligament, and it was hard to repair in the congested and difficult-to-access high-radiation area. There were frequent debates on whether to

[4]The end shield of a PHWR type of reactor is a vital structural component.

keep the reactor running or to permanently shut it down. But keeping the reactor running was important, not only for the credibility of the nuclear programme but also for our capability in managing the programme at that stage, when there were only a few operational power reactors.

Ultimately, a committee was set up under the chairmanship of N.B. Prasad, an early stalwart who worked on reactors and directly reported to Dr Bhabha while he was in BARC. It had other stalwarts like Brahm Prakash, M.R. Srinivasan, and P.R. Dastidar as members. The committee's debates were so loud and intense that I used to hear reverberations from where I sat. Several fixes were engineered to extend the life of the reactor. Today, the reactor is in extended shutdown. Of course, we now have a large number of operating PHWRs and so the issue has been significantly diluted.

Even as the commissioning work for Dhruva was in full swing, the Nuclear Power Board (NPB) had just started design work for a 500 MWe PHWR. I had chalked out a detailed development plan for the reactor that was to be implemented at BARC. Dr Ramanna proposed that BARC and Nuclear Power Corporation of India Limited (NPCIL) should jointly work on the development of the new project. An office space was created in BARC for the team to work together. I was expected to shift and work from there. I was to continue to remain on the rolls of BARC and work for NPB. S.L. Kati of NPB, who was leading the project, was not in favour of this arrangement and wanted me to be transferred fully to NPB. He consulted S.M. Sundaram of BARC, who had led the Dhruva project. Sundaram was apparently not very receptive, as my transition to NPB did not take place.

But this was not the only time this happened. Given my inherent interest in the design of nuclear reactors, in addition to my efforts at the time of joining BARC, I came close to joining this group involved in designing and setting up power reactors on a number of occasions.

P.R. Dastidar, to whom I used to report back then, would tell me that NPB was asking for me to work for them full-time, but BARC was not willing to spare me. Dastidar was a sport and told me that if I was interested, I could take a transfer. I told Dr Ramanna, who was still the Chairman, that I was equally comfortable being posted at BARC or NPB, and could continue to work for both organizations. All through my career I have always worked under more than one superior at a time, and managing all of them simultaneously had not been difficult, although it was stressful. However, as before, I was not transferred and remained in BARC.

When Power Projects Engineering Division (PPED)[5] was to be set up in 1967, applications were invited from interested scientists and engineers. Many engineers from RED also applied. I too was keen to switch over to PPED, and submitted my application. KSS questioned me as to why I wanted to leave. I replied that although reactor-related development work was going on in RED at that time, it was not challenging enough. Those were early days and development was more open-ended, with no clarity on what would ultimately see the light of day. He told me that since I had submitted the application, he was duty-bound to forward it, but would impress upon Meckoni that I was better retained in BARC. I went to Meckoni to plead my case. I protested that while everyone else was being allowed to go, I was being held back. He tried to pacify me by saying that I had

[5]PPED was set up under DAE to pursue implementation of the nuclear power programme. The reactor design section of RED, BARC, was shifted to be a part of PPED. PPED later became Nuclear Power Board (NPB) and finally Nuclear Power Corporation of India Limited (NPCIL), a public sector company, in 1987.

the Stress Analysis Laboratory under my control. I retorted that I had been made the storekeeper of the Stress Analysis Laboratory, and no worthwhile programme was underway. He then countered that I was free to make my own programme if I stayed back, to which I replied that while I could think of many things to do, there was no value in doing them if they did not fall within the ambit of the main programme of the Department. But my arguments did not cut ice with him.

My desire was partially realized, although in a different way, when I became Director, BARC, in the year 1996. The Director of BARC also happens to be a member of the board of NPCIL, which had come into existence by then. Later, as Chairman, AEC, I again had a deep involvement in the matters of NPCIL. My passion has always been the design of reactors. It really did not matter whether I was at BARC or NPCIL. In retrospect, I feel that it served my interests to remain at BARC. I have often been asked whether I would have risen to become Chairman, AEC, had I switched to PPED or NPB or NPCIL. I have strong conviction that DAE recognizes merit, and I would have perhaps occupied the high chair in any case. However, had I been in NPCIL, I would not have been able to contribute to the national strategic programme. Being in BARC, I had the opportunity to work for both the strategic as well as the nuclear power programme. I once again feel obliged to remember and thank my mentor, Subramanyam, who had a gut feeling that it would serve both me and the organization best if I remained in BARC.

INTRODUCING THORIUM IN POWER REACTORS

After completing Dhruva, my focus was back on heavy water reactors for power production. We began exploring opportunities for utilizing thorium in PHWRs, similar to the way it had been used in CIRUS as well as in new innovative heavy water reactor configurations, which could address safety concerns that had arisen as a result of the Chernobyl accident in a more fundamental way.

Thorium utilization had been a key objective of the department. Several aspects of thorium were being examined analytically as well as experimentally by different groups in BARC and in other units of DAE. This has been an ongoing programme and has led to fabrication of thorium fuel, irradiation in reactors, reprocessing of irradiated fuel to separate uranium-233, and building small reactors using uranium-233. Dr Kamala Balakrishnan, a reactor physics expert on thorium, used to explore reactor physics aspects wherever there was an opportunity.

Every time a new PHWR power plant was made operational, one needed to use depleted uranium bundles in the fresh reactor core to achieve full reactor power from day one. Using thorium for this purpose instead was an opportunity to irradiate thorium in power reactors on a large-scale without any additional penalty, as only the excess reactivity of the fresh core, which had to be suppressed anyway, was being used. Kamala worked out the detailed configuration for locations of thorium bundles in a way that would meet our requirements without significantly affecting the worth of the reactivity elements. We made a proposal for use of thorium in the PHWRs for the purpose of power flattening.

As a next step, I wanted Nuclear Fuel Complex (NFC) to fabricate a few thorium bundles to be irradiated in the PHWRs. When I approached K. Balaramamoorthy, CE of NFC, he said he had already faced strong opposition from Dr Srinivasan, who apparently had been convinced by some experts that introducing thorium in PHWRs for power flattening was not feasible. He, too, was a bit apprehensive about introducing thorium in his fabrication plants, for fear of mix-up of uranium and thorium. There was no other fuel fabrication facility in the country where

I could go. In one meeting, Dr Srinivasan went so far as to threaten that if he ever heard the word 'thorium' again, that would be the end of me. It was only when Dr Iyengar became Chairman, AEC, that the idea got traction and use of thorium bundles for power flattening in fresh PHWR cores became a norm. This gave us valuable experience on the large-scale use of thorium in power reactors, and also made a significant addition to our uranium-233 inventory for pushing the thorium programme forward.

CREATION OF AHWR

Post the Chernobyl accident, there was a lot of discussion about the safety of nuclear power plants. I myself chaired a committee to look at PHWR as a system in the context of that accident. As a result of the detailed work, it was established that PHWR was much safer than other reactors. Additionally, several safety augmentations were brought in to further strengthen the system wherever it was felt important. Yet, I realized that the problem of public trauma caused by large-scale displacement of people following a severe accident cannot be solved by quantitative safety arguments based on low probabilities or slight consequences. I understood that the issue of such trauma or a disaster syndrome caused by a severe nuclear reactor accident is not exactly identical to the issue of nuclear reactor safety. What we needed was a reactor that was immune, to the maximum extent possible, to core heat up, making isolation between the reactor and the public domain unnecessary. I also felt that we should be able to realize such an objective by clever configuration design using currently available technologies. This would enable such an objective to be realized much sooner than acquiring an entirely new technology.

Further, given our long-term interest in thorium, we could configure such a reactor system around thorium as a fuel, delivering most of the energy produced by the reactor. Thorium could add to the safety strength of the reactor as a result of its superior thermo-physical properties. This was the origin of the Advanced Heavy Water Reactor (AHWR). Along with Kamala, we managed to evolve this concept, which was perhaps the first design exercise where physics and engineering disciplines worked hand in hand as a single group.

R.K. Sinha, who had been working with me right from the beginning, led the work of detailing the AHWR design. A massive development project was launched. The design had also been put through an independent review. The AHWR has robust safety strengths of unprecedented magnitude, including the ability to deal with malevolent acts. The reactor can be deployed in the relatively lower levels of technological infrastructure that prevail in several developing countries. A lot of thinking has also gone into organizing the fuel cycle for the AHWR.

The momentum gained on the AHWR programme had to be temporarily slowed down because of competing demand on plutonium, also needed for the driver fuel for the Prototype Fast Breeder Reactor (PFBR), discussed below. Now that we are past that stage, I do hope that the construction of the AHWR can begin without further delay. A version of the AHWR fuelled by thorium and Low Enriched uranium fuel (AHWR300-LEU) has also been worked out, primarily for the export market. The system, in my view, is a perfect technological response to the need of providing high levels of safety and security assurance for large-scale deployment of nuclear energy. To me, this seems indispensable in addressing the threat of climate change.

MORE MILESTONES

During the early '80s, I also had more than one brush with the submarine programme. A.K. Anand was in-charge of the programme. At that time, plutonium was being considered as fuel for the reactor. I felt that the use of plutonium for a submarine reactor would not be appropriate. I conveyed my concern to P.R. Dastidar, our Director at the time. One day, he called me and said, 'Kakodkar, you go to Europe, visit industries there and figure out the manufacturing technology for reactor pressure vessels.' T.K. Ghosh, the in-charge of the DAE liaison cell at Paris, organized an intense programme of visits to a dozen facilities in Europe, to be accomplished within ten days. It was a rewarding experience for me, because I saw the manufacturing of large components like pressure vessels, steam generators, pumps, etc. including processes like forging, cladding and welding.

When I visited Klockner Werke in Germany, the makers of pressure vessels, I was asked why I travelled all the way to Germany to see the equipment—Heavy Engineering Corporation Limited (HEC) had similar equipment at their factory in Ranchi. I had never been to HEC, so upon my return I visited the factory. On the flight to Ranchi, I met a gentleman who was also going to HEC. We were lodged in the same guest house, so I got curious and asked what brought him to HEC. He replied that he was representing a private firm and had come to place orders for rollers for material handling. He required simple rollers, just about a metre long and a few centimetres in diameter. He wanted a few hundred of them.

Our contact at HEC was the commercial manager, who showed more interest in negotiating the orders for those simple rollers than in engaging with us. When our turn came, I commented that HEC was such a large engineering factory, but seemed more interested in making ordinary rollers than fabricating specialized forgings. The commercial manager expressed his helplessness, 'Sir, what to do? We have no orders.'

I then explained that we had come looking into the possibility of fabricating pressure vessels for nuclear reactors. We were directed to meet the two experts (Majumdar and Mule) on the shop floor. They refused outright, saying that they would not be able to make such vessels. When I told them that they had equipment similar to the ones at Klockner Werke, where nuclear reactor pressure vessels were being made, and that engineers in Germany had told me that HEC could make this product, they had no excuse. Reluctantly, they agreed to give it a try. Over a period of time and after a lot of trials, they finally succeeded in making the vessels for the Indian nuclear submarine programme.

However, the issues around sustaining such critical technological capability in our industry, so painstakingly built, still daunt us. It is unlikely that this, and many other such technologies that are important in several other sectors of national endeavour and economy, would survive market competition. There is a need for a broader national policy to facilitate their growth in the domestic competitive market. Actions in tandem by several government departments are necessary for this purpose.

My further involvement with the submarine programme took place when I became Director, BARC. While plutonium had long ago been changed to uranium as fuel for the reactor, the fuel matrix had still retained oxide fuel. The land-based prototype of the submarine was being set up at Kalpakkam with uranium oxide fuel. I felt that with oxide fuel, the prototype would not adequately represent the performance features demanded of such a platform. I told the physicists to run the calculations for the metallic matrix (which was almost ready by that time) without altering the basic core design. They did so and confirmed the feasibility of changing over to the new fuel matrix. The fuel designers went back to the drawing board to rework the engineering design. Initially several members of the team were upset about this mid-course correction, but I think they were all convinced, upon retrospection, that the value of the prototype facility had gone up tremendously. The new fuel was ultimately used in the prototype reactor.

The work at Kalpakkam was being led by Sekhar Basu. Apart from BARC, members from the Indian Navy were also part of the project. As the project approached commissioning stage, the number of people at Kalpakkam, including Navy personnel, started swelling. A joint management structure for the facility needed to be developed and put in place. The Navy wanted the overall control of the facility. This was not acceptable to me, since the facility was located in a DAE complex, with several other facilities that were also handling radioactive material. From the perspective of radiological safety, the entire site had to be under a single command. That command had to be with DAE, since DAE would be answerable in any event that impacted the public domain. I then approached Dr Kalam, who was the Scientific Advisor to the Defence Minister and overall head of the Advanced Technology Vessel (ATV) project. We held long discussions with him and ultimately convinced him about the right management structure for the facility. Without making anyone unhappy, he quietly settled the issue. DAE had the overall control, with Basu being the man calling the shots. The prototype went critical on 11 November 2003—A. K. Anand's sixty-fourth and my sixtieth birthday—and it was made functional after several experiments. Later, Arihant also became operational. The programme is now proceeding on track.

In 1981, a Prototype Fast Breeder Reactor (PFBR) Working Group was appointed in which I was a member. The working group was tasked with suggesting a basic configuration for the PFBR. There was a major debate regarding the fuel to be adopted. Work was already ongoing on developing carbide fuel for the Fast Breeder Test Reactor (FBTR) being built at Kalpakkam. Recognizing the importance of short doubling time in a fast reactor programme, there was a strong opinion that we should move forward on the first step—advanced fuel development—which was already being taken in the form of development of carbide fuel. Nitride and metallic fuels were other choices under consideration. But there was a contrary opinion, to which I also subscribed. The PFBR was meant to be a commercial prototype, requiring good performance of the fuel in the reactor as well as in the fuel cycle, in tandem with the reactor. It was therefore prudent to adhere to the well-proven oxide fuel. This choice was not available for FBTR because of issues related to oxide fuels with high plutonium concentration. But the advanced fuels, including carbide fuels, could be adopted only after making our capability in fuel cycle technology robust. There was intense debate on the possible adverse impact of the long doubling time of oxide fuel on India's second stage power programme. After a long debate, I managed to convince everyone that the growth of the second stage programme in the early phase would be dependent on the ability of feeding plutonium from the first stage, rather than the fuel doubling time in the second stage. There was thus a time window during which the advanced fuel development could be taken to the robust level required before its actual deployment, without any adverse impact on the growth of the programme. This was the more prudent route. It was thus decided to adopt oxide fuel for PFBR. Later, after I became Chairman, AEC, we also decided to short close different options on advanced fuel and froze the choice of metallic fuel for future fast breeder reactors. We must now accelerate this development with a view to adopt metallic fuel for the second stage of the nuclear power programme as early as possible.

At the time I became Chairman, AEC, PFBR was still in the development stage. It was clear that the time was ripe for launching the second stage programme, although several weak links yet remained to be addressed. We needed a good vehicle to implement the fast breeder programme beside the Indira Gandhi Centre for Atomic Research (IGCAR)—the design and development centre—which would need to focus on furthering the second stage programme development. This led to the creation of the Bharatiya Nabhikiya Vidyut Nigam (BHAVINI), the second nuclear power company in DAE dedicated to fast reactors. Unlike the first stage, where the reprocessing of spent fuel need not be done concurrently with the operation of the reactors, the second stage is heavily dependent on reprocessing, both for their initial fuel supplies as well as for their regular operation. In order to bring in the necessary robustness in the operation and performance of reprocessing and recycle plants, significant restructuring of the back-end of fuel cycle activities was carried out. Sekhar Basu did an excellent job of improving performance in operation and project activities connected with recycle plants. A separate Nuclear Recycle Board was created to sustain these activities with a degree of industrial-scale efficiency. The beginning of this restructuring was accompanied by much pain. It is a matter of satisfaction that the strategy worked and has produced good results.

Talk about Accelerator Driven Subcritical Reactor Systems (ADSS) had also gained momentum around this time. This was of particular interest in the context of thorium. Apart from immunity with respect to criticality accidents, such systems meant potential for greater breeding on account of availability of neutrons of non-fission origin. As and when such a possibility is realized, one could assure growth of thorium systems independent of having to build large fast reactors. Whether this could be a route to hasten deployment of thorium on a large-scale was an interesting prospect to be explored. We thus explored AHWR cores in which one could incorporate spallation neutron sources driven by proton beams from an accelerator. The ideas, discussions and analysis work culminated in the conclusion that one could start with an AHWR as a super-safe power reactor, delivering around two-third of its energy from in-situ-bred uranium-233. The driver for such a configuration can, over a period of time, be changed from externally fed fissile material to spallation sources, or even a one-way coupled two-region core. While all this had to await the development of rightly capable proton accelerators, and the specifications for such an accelerator could be significantly moderated with the two-region core, we were sure that we could now go ahead with detailing of the AHWR. It had a full justification of its own, but could well be an important platform for further developments in the Indian atomic energy programme.

CHAPTER 4

Reactor Repair and Rehabilitation

RAPS END SHIELDS

Sometime around 1984-85, Dr Ramanna asked me if it was a good idea for NPB to permanently shut down unit one of RAPS. The proposal had emerged as there were frequent equipment failures in the reactor, particularly the end shield. He wondered if it could be used for something else. I replied that if we had a reactor, we could use it for a variety of purposes. Dr Ramanna then asked me to meet Dr Iyengar, who had a different take. He observed that the leakages were taking place in the top half of the core—so why not run the reactor at half power using the bottom half of the channels? It would become a kind of semi-circular reactor—half a cylinder. I agreed that it could work that way as well. K.R. Srinivasan made reactor physics calculations and I designed the engineering part. However, this methodology was not implemented. The leaking channels were mechanically plugged once again and the reactor ran at 100 MW (50 per cent) power for quite some time thereafter.

At that time, the nuclear power programme was not large and

scrapping an entire power reactor would have badly affected the programme's image in the public. The taxpayer would think that nuclear power was a loss-making proposition. I recollected the visit of Ostman of Atomic Energy of Canada Limited (AECL) to India earlier, when he had made a prophetic statement, 'RAPS-1 is your flagship reactor. For a fleet, the flagship should not be allowed to sink.' I narrated this to Dr Ramanna. The reactor may not have been operating at significant enough power to generate money, but it provided an opportunity to learn to repair reactors. We would not have gained such capability otherwise. The idea of scrapping the reactor was shelved.

The RAPS-1 end shield also had to be repaired quite a few times. End shields are drum-like structures made of nickel steel, one each on either end of the calandria.[6] Cracks had been developing on the tube sheet. In the early stage, some colleagues from BARC had suggested plugging the leaks using zinc polysilicate. H.S. Gadiyar, a corrosion engineer from the Materials Group, BARC, was alarmed when he came to know about it. The proposed method would generate hydrogen, which would aggravate the problem of cracking of steel at the crack tip. He tried to raise concerns about this repair methodology but was brushed aside. So he approached me for support.

A. Krishnan of PPED, which later became NPB and finally NPCIL, was in charge. In fact, Sundaram (the then Director of the Materials Group), Gadiyar, Krishnan, I and a few others went to see M.R. Srinavasan, then the Director of PPED, at his departmental

[6]The calandria of the PHWR is a horizontal drum-like structure holding about three hundred coolant tubes, which is the heart or the core of a PHWR reactor. The fuel bundles are loaded in these coolant tubes and heavy water flows across. The nuclear reaction takes place in the fuel, heating the bundles and in turn raising the temperature of flowing heavy water. The heated heavy water is used to generate steam. This steam then runs the turbine to generate electricity. The calandria is also filled with heavy water called the moderator.

residence at Zerlina in Malabar Hills. That happened to be a Deepawali day. I had to face the wrath of the seniors present in the meeting as I opposed the sealing of the end shield with zinc polysilicate. I was convinced by Dr Gadiyar's apprehension. We eventually prevailed in stopping that method of repair, and mechanical sealing was finally adopted to stop the leaks. Some more leaks developed later and were sealed in the same manner. The reactor has had a chequered history of operation due to frequent leaks and repairs.

MAPS REHABILITATION

At RED, BARC, we were closely associated with the nuclear power programme and would generally get to know about the happenings at NPCIL. One day, we came to know of a leakage in the calandria vault of one unit of the Madras Atomic Power Station (MAPS) located at Kalpakkam.

Initial investigations pointed towards leakage of moderator water in the calandria vault, which was a cause for concern and the first indicator of a potentially major problem, whose contours were yet unknown. The internals in the calandria are numerous and assembled in a complex geometry. To identify and get to the location of the failure was not easy. Access to the inside of the calandria was treachourous. The very high radiation field inside the calandria made investigation even more difficult. At RED, we were running a programme for development of gadgets and systems for the repair and maintenance of reactors. We had developed a vision system, a kind of laparoscope, which could be inserted inside the reactor to examine the internals and assess the damage. However, it was not meant to work in very high radiation. Normal glass turns opaque in radiation this high, thus losing its transparency. Thus the images were not clear, but we found out that the inlet manifold of the moderator circuit had failed and its pieces were lying strewn around. This in itself was serious enough, but to compound the misery, soon it occurred in the second unit of MAPS as well.

One day, Dr Srinivasan—Chairman, AEC by then—called me and expressed his concern about the failures at MAPS. He wanted to set up a committee, with me as Chairman, to solve the problem. I told him that the committee would need executive powers, and as I was not from MAPS or NPCIL headquarters, I did not fit in. He assured that the committee would be empowered and would not be handicapped in any way. It was then constituted with experts from NPCIL, MAPS, BARC and NFC, and me as its Chairman. We had to understand the severity of the damage and the reasons for failure, then work out a strategy for repair and eventually make a safety case to get the reactors started.

We began by making some contraptions for remote visual examination and working inside the calandria. A giant laparoscope was made by R.K. Sinha. M.S. Ramakumar, the robotics and remote handling expert, also developed a mechanical manipulator for working at the repair location. We realized that we needed a better vision system and, if available, better remote handling manipulators or robotics. Dr Srinivasan was eager to solve the problem at the earliest and told us to visit vendors in Europe and scout for suitable equipment. Accordingly, Rajagopal and I were to be deputed abroad. One day, I was in Old Yacht Club (OYC) in Colaba, Mumbai, where the secretariat of the Department of Atomic Energy is located, for a discussion with Dr Srinivasan. I also had to collect administrative clearances and foreign exchange for the travel. In those days, this required permission from the Reserve Bank of India and involved a lot of paperwork. At OYC, I bumped into Dr Iyengar, the Director of BARC. He asked me what I was doing there, and when I explained about the visit and that I was pursuing paperwork to travel abroad, he shot back, 'Why should they waste your time on administrative matters, foreign exchange, etc? Let the administration deliver it to you. You focus on your task. This kind of mundane matter should not bother you. Do not waste your time on such things.' I returned to my home in Anushaktinagar in the evening. The plan was that if I got my papers and foreign exchange, I would fly out the same night, else postpone my departure to the next date. I had informed the staff at OYC dealing with these matters of the same, and sure enough, by evening, the papers and currency were delivered to me at my residence. When I met Rajagopal at the airport, he asked me what I had said at OYC to get my clearances so fast. As it turned out, everyone at the office wanted to ensure that they were not the cause for delaying the travel. My casual linking of my departure date with the availability of the papers and foreign exchange, given the seriousness of the matter, had spread like wildfire and ironically underscored the urgency of the situation. The bureaucracy had gone into overdrive and quickly cleared all paperwork necessary for our travel.

We met vendors in Britain and France and narrowed down on M/s Visionics of France, who had a system that could work in low-radiation fields. It was designed for visual examination, and we requested them to build something that could do the repair work as well. M/s Visionics visited the site and succeeded in taking better pictures of the failure region than we had. But they could not make systems for repair work. We were left to do it ourselves.

R.K. Sinha of RED made a long-articulated arm with a gripper at the end. The arm could be inserted through the 10 cm opening and was robust enough to lift and manipulate heavy objects held at its tip. At first, we thought of using a cutter to cut broken loose parts into small pieces and retrieve them through the available opening. But the cutter did not work, as it could not exert adequate force at the tip. Luckily for us, the gripper had enough strength for lifting. We studied the calandria drawings and found that there were pockets at the end, which could safely store the broken parts and cause no further harm. The debris inside the calandria was thus cleared.

With the debris removed, the next hurdle was to explore safe circulation of moderator water. In the reactor, the moderator heavy water enters the calandria through the inlet manifold (which had failed) and goes out through the outlet manifold, both located inside the calandria. The reactor also has a dump tank at the bottom of the calandria, which is used during reactor shutdown for dumping the heavy water. With the inlet port damaged beyond repair, we decided to reverse the flow as a temporary fix. The heavy water would now enter from the outlet port and drop into the dump tank, from where it would be taken out. The reverse flow, while feasible at low power, placed limitations on operating the reactor at full power. This was due to radiation heating, buoyancy effect, temperature distribution and other parameters. B.K. Dutta made calculations of flow and temperature distribution at different power levels, and assessed a safe power level at which the reactor could be operated. I requested A.K. Chandra, who had developed a digital recorder, to install it at the time of reactor start-up so that the stability of moderator heavy water flow inside the calandria could be assessed with external measurements. Based on detailed assessments, it was decided to start the reactor with power initially limited to 50 per cent, i.e. 100 MWe. Accordingly, regulatory approval was sought, and we were all set to get the reactor on stream. And then came the twist.

K.S.N. Murthy, Director, Operations at NPCIL headquarters in Mumbai, was a dear friend. The evening before I was to leave for Kalpakkam for the start-up, his driver came to my home to deliver a piece of paper. It was a copy of a telex from Ostman of AECL, who had been informally consulted by someone in NPC on restarting the reactor after reversing the flow of the moderator. (It may be noted that the first PHWRs at Kota in Rajasthan were built in collaboration with Canada. Canada had similar reactors.) Ostman's message said that they did not think that it was a good idea to run the reactor with reverse flow of moderator heavy water. There was no remark by anyone on the Indian side. Immediately, I rang up Murthy and asked him what the NPC thought, as far as the plan to restart the reactor the next day was concerned. There was dead silence at the other end. When I pressed, he said, 'I sent it to you since I thought you should know.' I replied that it was nice of him to say so, but the reactor belonged to NPC. I was at best an external consultant. What was I supposed to do in the circumstance? It seemed to me that the management was against the solution. Murthy left it to me to decide. I told him I was going ahead, and his only reply was that he was not opposing my decision. And so I landed at Kalpakkam the next morning.

I met Rangarajan, project director at MAPS, and narrated my conversation with Murthy. Apparently, he already knew of it as Murthy had apprised him of the telex. I told Rangarajan that Murthy had not given me a straight answer, but since he was the man in charge at the site, I wanted him to take a stand. My intention was not to pressurize him. I did have the safety clearances, but the owners of the reactors had to make the prima facie decision. Rangarajan replied that he was keen to make an attempt; the reactor was dead in any case. With Rangarajan on board, we began making preparations for start-up. But it was now time for some more hiccups, albeit of different kinds.

S.R. Paranjpe, Director, IGCAR, barged in. During the

course of the rehabilitation work, he had offered to chip in. I had accepted his colleague in the team, essentially from the perspective of pursuing redundant analytical approaches, which could make the solutions more robust. Now, taking an about turn, Paranjpe said that if we were deciding to start the reactor based on calculations done by IGCAR, then IGCAR was not to be held responsible. This made me furious. I told him in no uncertain terms that I was not dependent on IGCAR. I had not asked for help in the first place. Moreover, I was guided by my own calculations, analysis and conviction. The previous night I had been put off by NPC, and now it was IGCAR. I turned to Rangarajan and asked him one more time whether he wanted to change his mind. He was firm and stood by me on starting the reactor.

Next, an operational issue popped up. The grid frequency[7] needed improvement so that the conditions for reactor start-up could be met. This would need load shedding. Rangarajan called grid management, requesting them to improve the frequency by shedding load. They enquired how much power MAPS reactor would contribute on start-up. When they were told it would be 50 MW (25 per cent) to begin with, they were amused. We were asking them to shed 100 to 150 MW of load, and in return offering just 50 MW. A lot of convincing had to be done by Rangarajan, citing national pride, nuclear energy, etc. Finally, they relented. The turbine maintenance was under Bharat Heavy Electricals Limited (BHEL). They also had to be taken on board. They too refused to consent, citing apprehensions about running the turbine for extended periods at 25 per cent power. I believed that BHEL engineers were being too bookish, and decided to

[7]For healthy operation of the equipment, particularly the turbine, in the nuclear power plant, the frequency of electric power supply is required to be within a narrow acceptable band.

start the reactor anyway. By then I was hardened enough, with such hurdles cropping up one after the other.

We started the reactor, constantly monitoring moderator water behaviour. I sat in the control room for nearly forty-eight hours, keeping a watch on the parameters. All went well and subsequently, we raised power to 50 per cent (100 MW). It was a big achievement for all of us. Once the reactor started operating, the same NPC that had indirectly opposed the reactor start-up began pushing for raising power to 100 per cent. I had seen detailed analyses and knew that with the temporary configuration the reactor was in, it would not be safe at 100 per cent power. I had to fight tooth and nail to convince them against doing so.

The next target was to find a permanent fix so that 100 per cent power was indeed realized. The answer lay in reverting the flow of moderator water within the calandria back to almost its original configuration. Since the inlet manifold was damaged, one needed an alternate mode of entry of moderator water. At BARC, we had begun development of sparger tubes[8] that could be fitted in the bottom lattice holes and serve as moderator inlets, more or less restoring the moderator flow pattern to the original one. Before the actual installation, the sparger tube had to be tested outside in the engineering hall. When we began trials, we found that for a good length of the tube, the water would not efface from the holes, necessitating a whirler to be designed and installed at either end of the tube. After successful trials, the next step was to obtain necessary safety clearances. Installing a sparger tube needed major modifications, as a hole had to be drilled

[8]A sparger tube is a long pipe with holes all along its length. This would evenly distribute moderator water into the calandria with sufficient protection to nearby calandria tubes, the way the original inlet manifolds were doing. The water would enter the sparger tubes, diffuse out of the holes, fill the calandria and exit from the outlet port.

through the thick shielding wall of the reactor. We went through all the procedures and installed the sparger tubes, thus finding a permanent solution for both units of MAPS. The reactors were back on stream, within six months of detection of the failure. Till date, both reactors are running well without any limitations on their power capacity on this account. I consider myself fortunate to be among the rare professionals who could undertake such a major reactor rehabilitation exercise. Some years later, when I visited MAPS, I could see the affection of the MAPS staff towards me. I was revered as a saviour of their reactors. Insights gained during the sparger tube development came in handy on two other occasions as well. Reactors at Narora were under commissioning, and the moderator water was being circulated. R.I.K. Murthy, an expert on vibration at RED, had gone there for vibration surveillance. On suspecting abnormality, he entered the vault through a narrow opening for inspection. He found out that at a T-junction, two pipes of smaller diameter coming from opposite sides were joining a larger pipe. The water jets coming from opposite sides were impacting against each other, leading to them swapping and banging on the walls in the larger diameter section. It was a water-flow problem, and if not rectified, could lead to major failure later. The problem was eliminated by a simple piping modification. Another case was about a sudden steam dump in the condenser at Narora Atomic Power Station causing internal damage to the dump pipe. Insights from the sparger tube design helped in quick rectification in this case.

LIFE MANAGEMENT OF COOLANT CHANNELS

Life management of coolant channels of heavy water reactors was recognized to be a key safety challenge soon after the major failure of the coolant channel at the Pickering-2 reactor in Canada

(Indian PHWRs are similar to the Canadian reactors). There were issues with both the material of the coolant channels (zircaloy-2) and the design of the garter spring supports. While the material of coolant channels in India was changed to zirconium-2.5 per cent niobium alloy from Kakrapar Atomic Power Plant (KAPP)-2 onwards, we had to cope with seven PHWRs that were already in operation with zircaloy-2 coolant channels. The challenge was to create a quantitative understanding of the damage mechanisms, maintain surveillance on some 2,100 coolant channels, carry out prompt repair wherever necessary, and assure safe operation till the available life was fully utilized and channels replaced in an orderly manner. This required a major engineering development to be accomplished and deployed concurrently while the reactors were operational. There was a lot of pressure, and to compound the problem, there were adverse comments from Canadians doubting our ability to handle the situation. They even brought IAEA in, citing safety concerns. While they had no intention to help, they were concerned about damage to their reputation in the event of another incident like the one at Pickering-2. The exercise, it seemed to me, had an agenda of force-closure of our operating units, citing safety concerns. A massive R&D project had to be launched to deal with all the issues on a war footing. A large part of BARC was involved in this effort. The risks (both the safety risk in case a channel was to rupture as well as the economic risk in case the reactors were to be shut down), were indeed very high. Some important mechanistic insights were developed through analytical and experimental work. Massive technology development work led to creation of systems for identification of channels that could be in distress, inspection of coolant channels, relocation of garter springs, other repair actions, assessment of health and remaining life of coolant channels, etc.

It is to the credit of my colleagues that the entire work could be done in an orderly manner and all seven reactors delivered energy to the maximum extent they could, with their coolant channels being replaced when due. Even the Canadians informally admitted to me that they realized there were aspects of Indian capability that were superior to theirs. As a matter of fact, once, while I was in Canada for a conference, they took me around their labs to show me their development projects, some of which were apparently out of bounds for their own personnel. Later, when I was Chairman, AEC, a high-level team from AECL even came to India to propose a collaboration to jointly market our 220 MWe PHWRs to third countries. I knew that this was at least in part because AECL was going through a difficult time. I was amused.

In light of such experiences, Dr Ramanna once expressed in a public forum, 'It is important that you do not get into a serious technical problem, but it is even more important that you are able to solve such problems if they arise.' Our dealing with a host of problems that arose at our plants has enabled us to build a robust capability, perhaps stronger than our capabilities in design and operation of the plants. Our self-reliance has become that much stronger.

CHAPTER 5

Nuclear Power on My Mind

One of the issues with nuclear power plants is their long gestation period for construction. That significantly adds to the interest burden and consequential higher tariff. As the design of the 500 MW PHWR was nearing completion, NPCIL got into deep financial trouble. It was created to enable access to the debt market for financing the nuclear power programme. At the time of the formation of NPCIL, it was agreed that the power programme would be financed through 50 per cent equity from government budgetary support and 50 per cent debt from the market, with equity flowing in first. To ensure faster programme implementation, it was decided that critical components that have long delivery periods should be procured in advance. The insight that had emerged from past experience was that project delays could be greatly eliminated if such critical items were ready at hand. Significant investments were made to procure these materials for both 220 and 500 MW PHWRs, with due approval of the Government. This procurement was financed through a loan borrowed by the company, with the expectation of timely financial approvals for various projects so that the loan could be returned once the budgetary support started flowing in.

TWISTS AND TURNS OF NPCIL

However, the annual budgetary support for NPCIL itself started dwindling. I recall a particular financial year when the annual budget dipped to as low as ₹168 crore. This was hardly significant as a budgetary equity support for any meaningful capacity-addition activity. Materials procured were lying idle, not leading to any productive assets. The mounting loan repayment burden had nearly pushed the company into a debt trap. The government had accorded administrative approval for Tarapur Atomic Power Station (TAPS) 3 and 4 (500 MWe PHWRs) in the Thane district of Maharashtra, but without any financial support. Y.S.R. Prasad, the then CMD, was a bold person. He refused to start work on the project unless the government granted financial sanction for equity support. Consequently, the project was hanging fire for a long time. By the time the financial sanction arrived and the work on TAPS 3 and 4 could be started, V.K. Chaturvedi, a dynamic leader, took over as CMD, NPCIL. The project galloped along, and it is remarkable that it was completed in a record time of less than five years.

The five-year construction period for TAPS 3 and 4, which were completed in the year 2005–06, was a feat that NPCIL can be proud of. But there is a strong need to be able to replicate this on a recurring basis. That would be a major boost to the scaling up of our nuclear power programme. The TAPS 3 and 4 project was also executed with a completion cost that was significantly lower than the approved costs. The project perhaps holds the rare distinction of seeking government approval to reduce project costs so that the consequent lower tariff could be notified. While the project was under construction, there was constant pressure to finalize power purchase agreements with prospective buyers such as State Electricity Boards (SEB). The SEBs, however, did not come forward, as they perceived the proposed tariff to be too high. I remember, as Chairman, AEC and Secretary, DAE, I had decided to simply remain silent and await project completion. By the time the project was completed, the tariff had become attractive enough and there was no difficulty in sealing the power purchase agreements.

The story of the 220 MWe PHWRs also evolved on similar lines. Two additional units were sanctioned by the government at Kaiga (Kaiga 3 and 4). These were to be financed with 50:50 debt-equity formula, as was the approved norm then (circa 2000–01). The manufacturing industry was in a slump at that time. Chaturvedi visualized that within the same approved equity, two more units at Rawatbhata, Rajasthan (RAPP 5 and 6) could be built by changing the debt-equity ratio to 70:30 and seeking quantity discounts from the manufacturing industry by ordering double the quantity. Through improved operation and construction performance, NPCIL's financial performance had grossly improved, and increasing the borrowing proportion was quite in order and consistent with the norm prevailing in the power sector at large. Then onwards, NPCIL also started equity financing of new power capacity out of its own resources without depending on governmental budgetary support. Now with much greater programme implementation at hand, NPCIL has a new challenge of raising adequate equity funding, both from the government as well as from other possible sources.

That was also the time when several other attempts were made to further improve the relative competitiveness of nuclear power. Heavy water is one of the most critical inputs for PHWRs. By then, gone were the days of heavy water shortage—we had become the world's largest producer of heavy water. The focus then shifted to producing heavy water more cheaply by making the processes more energy efficient. The Heavy Water Board took up several small projects to enhance energy efficiency. These projects had short payback periods. As a result, the plan outlay could be recycled to implement a much larger energy efficiency enhancement programme. We also looked at the way heavy water figures in the tariff structure of nuclear power. These efforts led to a significant reduction in tariff for nuclear power.

LONG-TERM HORIZONS

By 2004, NPCIL and BHAVINI were together constructing nine units simultaneously. One could visualize that we were ready to start implementing a large-scale nuclear capacity addition programme. Now, with a much larger capacity addition programme on the anvil, NPCIL would of course need to find equity funding from the government and other possible sources. In order to figure out the niche area for nuclear energy in the larger power development plans of the country, a detailed study was organized to look at the power scenario over five decades. Although such long-term horizons for planning processes in the power sector were previously unheard of in our country, they were necessary to figure out the effects of fuel and technology transitions—which are necessarily long-term phenomenon. The results of this study were later incorporated in the integrated energy policy that was prepared by the Planning Commission in the year 2006. But as we were preparing to embark on an ambitious nuclear power programme, it hit yet another roadblock.

Natural uranium, the fuel for the Indian PHWRs, was being sourced indigenously from the mines at Jadugoda and other locations in the state of Jharkhand. Uranium Corporation of India Limited (UCIL), a public sector undertaking under DAE, is engaged in mining and milling of uranium. Meghalaya has large reserves of uranium and we were banking heavily on that for enhancing uranium supply, which was needed for the expanding programme. UCIL, in its wisdom, thought that Domiasat in Meghalaya being a remote area, in-situ leaching of the ore would be preferable.[9] After a couple of years, UCIL concluded that local geology was not suitable for in-situ leaching. In the meantime, opposition from local residents and activists grew, and experimental activities and pilot mining too came to a standstill.

Another deposit, of upto 15,000 tonnes of uranium, was also identified in Tummalapalle in the state of Andhra Pradesh. Here, too, the ore was considered difficult to leach and was abandoned. The mine at Turamdih in Jharkhand was also abandoned halfway, perhaps at the prospect of Domiasat yielding rich ore and being more economical. Futile attempts were made to extract uranium from phosphate minerals as well. On one side, uranium supply was dwindling; and on the other hand, the reactors, which were now operating well, needed an enhanced feed of natural uranium fuel. The reactors were thus being forced to operate at a lower capacity factor, meaning that they were generating less electricity—at the risk of financial loss to NPCIL.

The options available to DAE were resolving the Domiasat tangle, exploring other avenues for uranium production, expanding uranium exploration and importing uranium. Each of these options had its own serious constraints. We were collectively discussing these issues and their potential resolution almost every week. Chaturvedi of NPClL and Chaitanyamoy Ganguly, the Chief Executive of NFC, formally wrote to me asking for uranium. I was the Chairman, AEC, and knew that the problem was not going to be solved by writing letters. It was a high-pressure situation for all of us, and some of us had started buckling.

---

[9]It is a chemical treatment carried out underground at the source location, with extraction of dissolved uranium.

I took Prime Minister Dr Manmohan Singh into confidence and apprised him of the grim situation. Prithviraj Chavan, the Minister of State in charge of DAE, an intelligent person, got a whiff of the crisis and probed deeper. He asked me why I was owning up to the crisis when it was not of my making. I replied that as I was occupying the chair in DAE, it was my responsibility to lead from the front. I explained that while a problem did exist, there was no need to panic. A plan to tide over the crisis was in place. Chavan hauled me up to the Prime Minister and told him about the uranium shortage. The Prime Minister looked at us with a calm face and showed no reaction, as he already knew the situation. Nevertheless, Chavan was concerned, as it could mean deep trouble. I was indeed in trouble, but there was no way I could shirk my responsibility.

The prospect of NPCIL going into red gave us all jitters, and we decided to work on multiple fronts. The reactor cores were reconfigured to yield maximum uranium utilization. This meant reducing the maximum obtainable capacity factor of power plants to 70 per cent, leading to higher energy output per tonne of uranium. This would reduce uranium consumption by almost half while remaining profitable, though at a much lower level. The research reactors CIRUS and Dhruva have low burn-up, meaning that the uranium burnt in those reactors still has a lot of juice left in the spent fuel. We decided to recycle this depleted uranium in power reactors. All scrap lying around in NFC, including in the ventilation ducts, was scrubbed and recovered to make fuel. Colleagues from NPCIL, NFC and BARC, ably led by S.A. Bhardwaj and R.N. Jayaraj, all rose to the occasion and successfully managed to tide over the crisis until uranium supplies could be enhanced. This was akin to a proverb in Marathi: *Daant korun pot bharne,* which roughly translates to 'using food particles stuck in the teeth to satiate one's hunger'. Such was the situation.

To enhance uranium supply, we decided to start the Banduhurang mine near Jadugoda, which is an open-cast mine; reopen Turumdih mine and set up an additional mill there; and also take up Tummalapalle mine and mill projects—in spite of all the challenges inherent in these projects. Ramendra Gupta, CMD of UCIL, led these efforts from the front on a war footing. He even brought Meghalaya's resources very close to the actual project stage by bringing all stakeholders together around a Meghalaya package, which included electricity lines, water supply, road construction and development of the area. I must mention contribution of S.K. Malhotra who did tremendous work on garnering local support for the Domiasiat project. He succeeded in organizing a public hearing at the project site—a difficult proposition given the challenging geographical and weather conditions and extremely hostile attitude of the Khasi Students' Union. We involved the local politicians and organized a meeting with the Prime Minister. We almost clinched the deal, but unfortunately it did not fructify because of the uncertain political situation in the state.

The challenge before us was far from over. Urgent steps were needed towards a paradigm shift to enhance the basic uranium resource in the country by mounting aggressive, technologically enabled uranium exploration activities. A special sanction was secured from the government to procure and deploy advanced aerial electromagnetic survey tools and state-of-the-art electromechanical drilling equipment on a massive scale. At the same time, realizing that an embargo on procuring the equipment might hit us at any time, BARC, IGCAR and other institutions were roped in for development of exploration equipment. I learnt later that such restrictions did surface.

In order to galvanize the efforts of the different units of DAE in managing this entire crisis, we had set up an informal weekly platform to review and coordinate all efforts. Managing power plants and their supply of uranium, mining and milling activities and exploration work were all freely and honestly discussed to explore if anything more could be done. In one of these discussions, A.B. Awati, a geologist in DAE, came up with a proposal to revive the Tummalapalle reserves. Although UCIL had given up on these reserves thinking that they were not leachable, a proposal was made to study the matter afresh and find a way out. Awati convinced V.P. Raja, Joint Secretary at that time in DAE, of the potential of this idea. Raja brought this to my notice. I set up a team of experts from UCIL, BARC and DAE under the leadership of Dr A.K. Suri to find a solution for the leaching of uranium from the Tummalapalle ore. The project was executed on a war footing and a pilot plant was set up at Jadugoda. The team ultimately succeeded in developing a process flow sheet for processing of uranium ore, culminating in the launch of the Tummalapalle project in the year 2007. Once it became possible to produce uranium there, exploration activity using advanced technology resumed. Today, that region alone is host to a uranium resource at least twice that of India's total uranium resources known earlier.

While these efforts were still short of meeting the entire requirements of the ongoing nuclear power programme, they helped the programme to survive. They paid off in terms of preventing NPCIL from sinking. Eventually, in addition to enhanced domestic production of uranium, we also succeeded in accessing uranium from the international market. This led to two streams of reactors, one under International Atomic Energy Agency (IAEA) safeguards and the other outside. The division was done in such a manner that requirements of the strategic programme could be fully met; all reactors could operate at their rated capacity and the three-stage nuclear power programme (envisaged by Dr Homi Bhabha) could proceed unhindered. The evolution of technology for the ongoing three-stage programme, and making it robust, would have to be achieved as a part of the programme outside IAEA safeguards. However, we would soon need to deploy the technology so developed to implement the three-stage concept even for programmes running with imported fuel that would be under IAEA safeguards.

With the uranium constraint removed, one could envisage the thermal power reactor programme to be much larger than 10,000 MWe—a limit that had been dictated by the domestic uranium resources that were known then. Large-scale thorium deployment could now be advanced by accelerating thorium-related development in parallel with the developments related to the second stage programme. Most importantly, I could see the de-shackling of the growth of the nuclear power programme. As I was preparing to demit office in atomic energy in 2009, I got a report on the 'way forward' compiled with the active participation of young people who had enough time left to implement it. S.A. Bhardwaj led this effort. Unfortunately, we have allowed precious time to be lost, particularly due to the clumsy handling of the issues related to civil nuclear liability by various stakeholders, which also crippled the ongoing domestic PHWR programme for some time. Ten years down the line, while the expected momentum is yet to be picked up, there does appear to be a silver lining in the clouds in the form of the sanction of a fleet of 10–700 MWe PHWRs, and progress on Russian Light Water Reactors (VVERs). Much more needs to be done to get closer to the target of 63 GWe by the year 2032—which I still believe is not impossible.

While I was battling the crisis in the nuclear power programme, another storm was brewing. The Comptroller and Auditor General of India (CAG) had carried out a performance review of DAE in 2009. The report had come down heavily on certain aspects of programme management. The auditors had visited NFC and observed that it had failed to construct the additional plants for fuel fabrication that had been projected as a part of the ongoing power programme. This was at a time when uranium was in short supply and adding fabrication capacity, which could be set up in a relatively shorter gestation period, would not make sense. Earlier, too, the CAG had objected citing blocked capital while there was an accumulation of the uranium stockpile as the power programme took its time to grow. I tried to argue that there was a dichotomy in the objections of CAG. When the department had uranium, it was being castigated for locking up government money, and when there was no uranium, the objection was on non-construction of additional fuel fabrication plants—an action that had actually avoided blocking of public money. The CAG also took serious note of power projects being sanctioned without adequate fuel linkages. I defended this by pointing out the large gestation periods involved in building of nuclear power plants and the relatively shorter gestation periods needed in setting up fuel fabrication plants. When there were a number of projects being implemented under the nuclear power programme, under difficult circumstances involving challenging domestic technology development and international embargoes, there was bound to be some slippage. It should be up to the overall programme manager to work on strategies that lead to optimum programme delivery. Accountability on individual project progress should not lead to compromise on the overall programme performance. I also felt that our vulnerabilities vis-à-vis uranium shortages being discussed in public could compromise further strategies to access uranium from international sources. The auditor, however, was in no mood to listen.

In addition to all transactional audits, occasionally the CAG conducts performance audits including those of research centres. The process involves people from the audit office going through all files and raising a set of queries that are then tossed to higher levels for responses, thereby making a value judgement on the performance of the institution. I proposed to the audit team that gaps in understanding were causing a lot of misplaced discussions and conclusions. I therefore offered that a team of knowledgeable independent scientists selected by CAG should carry out the performance audit review. Initially, the idea appeared acceptable and we were all set to begin the process in that mode. However, at the last minute, the whole plan was set aside and the process went through as originally planned.

CHAPTER 6

The Making of a Nuclear Weapons State

Sometime in 1972, Meckoni, our Group Director, asked me to meet BARC Director Dr Raja Ramanna. He did not say anything specific but conveyed that it was an urgent matter and asked me to meet him at the earliest. Dr Ramanna directed me to meet Dr Chidambaram, who was working in the Physics Group under Dr Iyengar. Dr Ramanna then asked me something strange. He enquired whether I had the habit of talking in my sleep. I replied that I could not possibly know that myself. He asked whether my wife had noticed anything. I said that while she hadn't mentioned anything of the kind thus far, that did not mean I did not talk in my sleep, and I would ask her. We then moved on to general talk—nothing specific—and that was Dr Ramanna's style. I had no clue about what was happening or why he wanted to see me. Before I left, he asked me to keep visiting him every once in a while. I assured him that I would be there at a moment's notice if he had need of me or had a job for me, but I would not presume to disturb him on my own. When he asked if I would never visit him unless he called for me, I said that I was very junior to him and would try to solve my problems by myself rather than getting the Director involved. He then tried a different approach and asked me to meet him at his house. I replied that this was even more unlikely. Nevertheless, if he called me, I would meet him anywhere. Finally, he told me to meet J.N. Soni as well, who was in-charge of the workshop in the Nuclear Physics Division (NPD).

Dr Chidambaram briefed me about the assignment. It was work related to the nuclear device for the PNE to be carried out at Pokhran. They were looking for a mechanical engineer for the design and fabrication of the device. He provided a lot of relevant information. After meeting him, I went to meet Soni in his workshop. They had been trying various methods, but not making much headway. P.R. Dastidar, who was working on control systems, had suggested that I should be inducted into the work. Soni was doing his best, but things had reached a point where a mechanical engineer was needed. I studied the problem and realized that many mid-course corrections were necessary. They were all put in place. At that time, I had also started working on the design of the Dhruva reactor. With the new assignment, my work expanded to three locations: my own engineering hall where reactor development (particularly PHWR and later Dhruva) was the focus, the Dhruva project office where the reactor design and project work was being executed, and the NPD workshop where the PNE work was being done secretly. Carrying out such an expanded multi-group, multilocational work programme was a challenge and a joy. It was also stressful, as working under different bosses at the same time is bound to be. Most importantly, the multiple assignments provided an excellent cover for the sensitive work.

At that time, IAEA had been running a programme on PNE experiments and had also been organizing conferences and meetings aimed at exploring possibilities such as digging big canals, creating lakes or breaking ore bodies to make them easier to leach, etc. Many such experiments were being carried out. Scientific papers were being written and presented at such conferences. India conducting a PNE was thus a perfectly consistent and legitimate exercise, and in line with the international efforts to develop peaceful applications of atomic energy.

However, the trigger for the decision by the government must have been the 1971 war that led to the creation of Bangladesh. The Seventh Fleet of the US, equipped with nuclear weapons, had entered the Bay of Bengal at that time. It is my inference that India conducting a PNE at that time must have been considered as a very meaningful act. In my assessment, India did not really want to develop nuclear weapons, despite concerns about her long-term security. The nuclear option had thus been kept open all along. After the 1974 event, however, the term PNE vanished from the IAEA lexicon and the world rallied around to punish India for doing something that was considered to be a prerogative of recognized nuclear weapon states alone. A global regime of nuclear embargo was clamped around India. Paradoxically, while significantly delaying the deployment of nuclear energy for India's growth—and indeed for the rest of the developing world—this had no impact on her strategic programme. This was a realization that dawned on the world only after India decided to do the tests again. Forced by the circumstances, India exercised its nuclear option and announced herself as a nuclear weapon state.

I began work on the design of the device, and in time, things came under control. Soon the preparation activities expanded. The Terminal Ballistic Research Laboratory (TBRL) at Chandigarh was actively involved in them from the Defence Research and Development Organisation's (DRDO) side. We had to visit TBRL frequently for long durations to coordinate interfaces between the work of the two institutions. This was both at the design level as well as the logistics level, including the planning and coordination of work at the Pokhran site. Our help was needed at many places. A lot of gadgets had to be fabricated. Team spirit was so high that individual, group or organizational boundaries and identities had all melted away. Every necessary task was performed without quibbles about whose job it was. The team had to necessarily be small, given the sensitivity of the project, comprising a few highly dependable and competent personnel. This meant that each one of us became a one-man battalion. Everything had to be done under suitable cover to maintain secrecy. For me, this was a big challenge—being accountable to multiple programmes and not letting anyone get wind of what I was doing secretly. This was indeed a great learning experience for me.

At Pokhran, an army regiment was busy preparing the site. This involved a wide range of activities. Digging of the shaft had started in full swing. Geologists, seismologists, control and instrumentation experts, health physicists and other professionals were all busy with their respective work. We were at the core of all these activities, having responsibility of the assembly and placement of the device itself.

My work required me to travel without leaving a trail. All relevant information was restricted and even Meckoni, to whom I was supposed to be reporting, did not know about my whereabouts. To his credit, Meckoni himself told me that I should not tell him anything. But others in my division at Trombay were not so charitable and were resentful. I never told anyone what I was working on to begin with, and now I would disappear for days or weeks without telling anybody. I would never travel directly to any destination. It would always be a circuitous route to avoid leaving clues or being tracked. I would usually travel under different aliases. Once, I was traveling as Prof. Rao.

A DRDO engineer was slated to meet me. As I was waiting for him, the fact that I was supposed to be Prof. Rao left my mind. Someone approached me and asked, 'Are you Prof. Rao?' I said no outright. Fortunately, he had probably seen me earlier and recognized me. In a hushed tone he said, 'Dr Kakodkar, I was supposed to meet you as Prof. Rao.' I remembered my alias, and we moved on.

Finally, the time came to prepare the test at the site. A lot of work was required. It was not possible to fabricate everything at the workshop in Trombay and then transport all of it to the site. Some items were fabricated elsewhere, including at Jodhpur, which is the largest city close to Pokhran. We reached the site weeks in advance. The amenities were scarce. Logistics was difficult.

Soni was about ten to fifteen years senior to me, and we made a great team. He was adept at handling people. For transport, we were given a dilapidated jeep. There were no cushions and we had to sit on a hard tin sheet. Travelling in the desert for long distances at the peak of summer, the jeep bouncing up and down over the dunes, was very uncomfortable and tiring with such seats.

One day Soni found out that a consignment of foam mattresses had arrived at the site. He asked the commanding officer to provide cushions in the jeep, and if that was not possible, to at least provide a mattress that could be cut up and refashioned into seat cushions. The commanding officer replied that the mattresses were meant for the senior and important officers who were expected to arrive soon. Soni was furious. He asked who these important persons were. The commanding officer took big names: 'Sethna, Ramanna, Nag Chaudhuri and other officers.' 'Never mind,' said Soni, 'I will take a mattress and tear it apart. You can report to anyone that I have taken a mattress to make cushions out of.' The commanding officer was a Lieutenant Colonel in the army. Soni impressed on him that we were scientific officers and in terms of grade, were equal, or even senior, to him. Just because we were doing manual work did not mean that we did not deserve equitable facilities. The argument did its job. The jeep had better cushions the next day onwards. Soni had done it.

One day, while travelling from the base camp at Pokhran to the site, which was a long distance away, our jeep broke down. On examining the engine, we found that the fan belt was torn and needed to be replaced. Getting a new fan belt or arranging alternate transport would easily have taken three to four hours. I decided to make a rope out of the shrubs growing around us and fashioned it into a belt. That allowed us to cover the remaining distance, saving the precious day. Such were the circumstances under which the work had to be carried out—very challenging, yet very enjoyable.

THE 'HO JAYEGA' MAN

Our main job at the site was integration. A shed next to the pit was erected for this purpose. We used to work in the shed as well as in the pit—making several trips up and down was a daily feature. One day, I discovered that the system meant for lowering the device lacked structural robustness. I pointed it out to Dr Iyengar, but he was in no mood to listen. He was in a hurry to get things done. When the device was actually being lowered in the shaft, the frame started visibly bending and twisting. I called Dr Iyengar and showed him what was happening. He panicked and asked whether we should stop. I said it need not be stopped at that juncture, but he should have listened to me when I had told him about it earlier.

We had our share of difficulties while assembling the device as well. Some of the people working with us began panicking and started reciting religious hymns. We had to tell them to maintain composure and focus on their work, so that others were not distracted by their panic. One day, we were late in completing the day's work and returned to the base around 11:30 PM in the night. Meanwhile, somebody had reported to Dr Ramanna that we were delayed because we were having difficulties. We found him anxiously pacing up and down. When he saw us, he asked what had happened. I replied that there had been some assembly difficulties, but everything had been solved successfully. He asked me what the difficulties were, and I replied that he wouldn't understand. I reassured him with the colloquial phrase, '*Ho jayega,*' meaning 'it will be done'. I used that phrase a number of times in the conversation that day. This led to Ramanna dubbing me 'the "ho jayega" man'. If Kakodkar said '*Ho jayega,*' that meant that it would be done. In many such moments of crisis, I have seen some people panic while others who stay calm and composed rise to the occasion. That day, I realized the importance of being trained as a hardcore engineer.

WHEN BUDDHA SMILED

After our job was done, we moved to the control room, which was located several kilometres away. Seshadri was carrying out the control-related activities. His job involved specially developed instrumentation and the laying of cables, which were running all over the place. He had also worked on the trigger. Since we had no more work to do, we simply parked ourselves on the sand outside the control room, which was small. Occasionally we would go inside to see how things were being done. Several of the team members started asking me how I felt about the whole exercise. I was calm, and explained that if we had done our jobs correctly, the experiment was bound to succeed. While everyone else seemed excited, I maintained my composure. And then, the countdown began. The button was pressed. The mound rose right in front of our eyes and went down. People started jumping with excitement. Everyone wanted to rush to the crater. Ramanna tried to restrain them himself by telling them that it was not scientific to do so and would destroy the evidence. Moreover, the personnel could place themselves in danger, as the ground had fractured and could cave in, leading to entrapment. Nobody was listening, and finally Ramanna had to shout to stop them from moving. One must always proceed scientifically.

The experience of Pokhran in 1974 was a great learning, generally in terms of a new programme domain but particularly in terms of the human dynamics that I witnessed before, during and after the tests. Working in a team, in extreme weather at the site and back in the less harsh environs of RED in BARC, the interpersonal relations that I experienced were eye-openers. And on a greater level, India grew in stature globally and the world realized that the country could not be ignored.

IN THE AFTERMATH

We had been briefed about the possible repercussions of the test: Its effect on our economy and the atomic energy programme, and the likely political reactions of different nations. The Canadians were working on the Rajasthan Atomic Power Project, but they left midway, abandoning the project. The test had come as a shock to them. While this is understandable, their reaction was a little too much.

One of the major fallouts of the Pokhran test was the disruption of the low-enriched uranium fuel supply for our US-supplied boiling water reactors at Tarapur. The Americans, who were contractually bound to supply the fuel, discontinued the supplies. Sethna was the Chairman of AEC at that time. He took a firm stand, while everybody in the government wanted to work out a compromise with the Americans and find an amicable way out of the tangle. Sethna maintained that it was the responsibility of the Americans to supply fuel. P.C. Alexander was the principal secretary then, who, much later (when he was governor of Maharashtra), told me that Sethna had showed extraordinary grit and stood up to the American pressure single-handedly. Sethna pushed for development of Mixed Oxide (MOX) fuel based on plutonium recovered from reprocessing of the spent fuel, to be used as alternate fuel for the Tarapur reactors. Facilities were created in the Department and a few assemblies were manufactured, and even underwent trial irradiation in the reactor. He readied the Department to recycle the spent fuel accumulated at Tarapur and at other locations in order to continue operation of the Tarapur reactors. However, the Americans worked out an arrangement with the French for supply of fuel to the Tarapur reactors for the remaining period of the contract. Subsequently, we also got fuel for TAPS 1 and 2 from Russia and other countries. However, getting fuel for Tarapur remained a matter of constant anxiety that ended only after we got Nuclear Supplier's Group (NSG) exemption.

While there was euphoria within DAE, in PPED (which later became NPB and finally NPCIL) there was significant concern on the adverse impact on the nuclear power programme. In BARC, too, some of my contemporaries in the reactor groups became jealous. They shared their concerns regarding the adverse impact of the technology embargo we would be subjected to, on the reactor programme. Being in BARC, they were not as vocal as their colleagues in PPED. Clearly, as a development community, the challenges before them (and me) had grown bigger.

After the initial euphoria of the test died down, PHWR-related work gained momentum. Though initially the test had created friction between BARC and PPED, over time the two came closer again. The cooperation between the two intensified as the vulnerabilities of dependence on outsiders became starkly visible. The importance of the motto of self-reliance became self-evident. The two organizations bonded like never before, and several things were accomplished. A large number of PHWR components were designed, developed and tested in BARC. These included the end fittings, coolant tubes, calandria tubes, garter springs, fuelling machines and many more.

India not only completed the reactors at Rawatbhata and Kalpakkam, which were under construction when the Pokhran experiment was being carried out, but also took up design and construction of new reactors. Although the programme did suffer delays, it moved confidently forward in spite of the global restrictions.

BACK TO POKHRAN

Negotiations on the Comprehensive Test Ban Treaty (CTBT) were underway. On the face of it, this was a part of the dialogue to further develop the global architecture to prevent spread of nuclear weapons. Conceptually, India had initially been in favour of it. The final draft, as it emerged, however, was a big departure from what India had visualized. Rather than moving towards total nuclear disarmament, the world was moving towards perpetuating the divide between nuclear haves and have-nots. Further, the text had an entry into force clause that required the signature and ratification of all forty-four countries listed as nuclear technology capable. India was one of them. Since the text was not acceptable, India voted against it. India's stand on the CTBT was famously articulated by late Ambassador Arundhati Ghose in 1996 in the

United Nations Assembly Hall thus: 'I would like to declare on the floor of this august assembly that India will never sign this unequal treaty—not now, nor later. As long as this text contains this article, Mr President, this treaty will never enter into force.' I remember that earlier, when CTBT negotiations were undergoing intense discussions, Arundhati Ghose had visited BARC. There was a broad-based discussion at the lunch table, where senior scientists were also present. Several technical aspects and ramifications in the Indian context were explained to her during these discussions. Much later, she told me how important that particular visit and discussion at BARC was in terms of greater clarity on the issues involved, and how it led to recalibration of our national approach in the matter.

CTBT was to enter into force 180 days after the date of deposit of the instruments of ratification by all forty-four nuclear technology-capable countries, but in no case could this be earlier than two years after its opening for signature. CTBT opened for signature in September 1996. Seventy countries, including the five nuclear weapon states, signed the treaty on the very first day. The number of signatories to the treaty was rapidly growing.

So far, we had maintained ambiguity with respect to our approach to the nuclear option. While India's sustained efforts towards making progress on total nuclear disarmament were not going anywhere, the security situation around India was worsening. Chinese aspirations to acquire global power status and move towards area dominance, along with their active support in equipping Pakistan with nuclear weapon capability, had been a matter of serious concern for some time by then. It was also clear that Pakistani nuclear weapons were under the control of its military. India had thus to be ready to deal with two nuclear adversaries on its borders. On top of this, with CTBT gaining traction, there was a grave danger of the international attitude towards India rapidly deteriorating. India had to deal with the issue on its own strengths. Each country has to be responsible for its own security, and time had come for India to exercise its nuclear option. As a matter of fact, exercising it was inevitable. It was clearly not tenable to block CTBT from being enforced while also remaining ambiguous about our own nuclear option. In a way, the global situation had forced it upon us. It was an evolution and not an overnight decision. Surely the decision must have required tremendous courage.

This was the background that necessitated India to carry out the 1998 tests. There was always awareness about the evolving situation, and preparations, although at a slow pace, were being pursued all along. In a manner of speaking, there was always a state of readiness. For DAE, this was a particularly trying period, as everything had to done on the basis of complete deniability.

TEST MATRIX: PUSHING THE ENVELOPE

Dr Ramanna had gotten two shafts dug up at Pokhran in the mid '80s. There would be occasional instructions to start preparing for the tests, and then, just as suddenly, to stop. The situation within the country had its own challenges. The resolve of the government at the centre to withstand international pressure in case of a nuclear test was a major factor. Alongside, there were discussions on the possible test matrix (the type and number of weapons to be tested) should the opportunity arise. DRDO was of the view that the miniaturized standard fission weapon design based on the 1974 PNE test, which had been developed, integrated and dummy-tested with missiles and aircrafts, should be qualified using the two available shafts. In DAE, we were of the view that we should push the envelope of our capability to the maximum possible extent, as no further opportunity to test was likely to arise in future.

It was apparent that nuclear weapon states would continue further advancements in nuclear weapons development even if the CTBT came into force. These advancements would be based on laboratory experiments, including sub-critical tests backed by computer simulation. Several nuclear weapon states at that time had actually announced their intentions to do so, and had managed to tweak the CTBT text suitably. There was also information that a side understanding had been reached between weapon states on the activities permissible to legally sustain further nuclear weapon development. It was therefore necessary to demonstrate a) thermonuclear weapon capability necessary for enlarged deterrence and b) to test out a dozen different ideas through a limited number of integral tests and validate them through experiment-analysis comparisons. This approach would not only demonstrate existing capability, but also allow further development. The constraint was that only two shafts were available. Constant external surveillance made the task of drilling additional big shafts difficult, if not impossible. With the CTBT debate heating up on one side and wavering of decision-making in the government on the other, the time available for necessary preparations was uncertain. Instead of digging new shafts, we decided to look around for abandoned deep-dry wells, where validation of low-yield (sub-kiloton[10]) tests could be done. Apart from being a practical way of achieving the objectives, this would also be a better demonstration of our computational capability. This approach would escape the peeping eyes of satellite surveillance, as minimal work was involved. A

[10]A test where the yield is restricted to less than a kiloton of TNT so that the test remains well contained, even if done in available wells

number of abandoned wells were identified and made ready. Simultaneously, the work of getting the thermonuclear device ready was in full swing, to ensure that we did not miss out on its testing.

I raised the issue of testing the thermonuclear device with Dr Kalam, who was the chief of DRDO and also the overall leader of this programme. DRDO was not keen and wanted to use both shafts to test the standard fission weapon that had been developed. We at DAE did not want to miss out on what could perhaps be the only opportunity to achieve thermonuclear capability as a part of the national nuclear deterrent. I pressed for inclusion of testing of the thermonuclear device in the test matrix. Kalam was presiding over the meeting, sitting as an umpire. He asked what the maximum yield would be, since the village Khetolai was located only a few kilometres away. It had to be protected from any damage. We had run calculations and concluded that the total yield would need to be limited to around sixty kilotons to prevent unacceptable damage to the village. However, the two existing shafts were not too far apart. If we used one shaft for a test, the other would most certainly be damaged. Conducting tests in both shafts simultaneously was thus unavoidable. With the yield of a standard fission weapon at 15 kilotons, the maximum permissible yield to successfully test the thermonuclear weapon thus had to be 45 kilotons. Kalam was unsure whether this could be done and was worried about the consequences of the yield turning out higher. After a long debate, finally, Kalam said, 'Anil, we are friends, but can you write it down that we can create a thermonuclear device with yield close to 45 kiloton and no more, and that the village of Khetolai would not suffer any damage as a result of testing it?' I agreed to put my neck on the block, and gave a duly signed, written note as asked for by Kalam. With that, Kalam agreed for the inclusion of the thermonuclear weapon in the test matrix.

The test matrix included a 15 kiloton standard fission package, a 45 kiloton thermonuclear package, and three sub-kiloton packages that incorporated a large number of ideas between them. A fourth sub-kiloton package was also readied, but there was no need to test it, as everything worked well. A physics team was led by S.K. Sikka. M.S. Ramakumar and D.D. Sood led the fabrication teams. G. Govindarajan and V.K. Gupta led the electronics & instrumentation and health physics teams respectively, and Vilas Kulkarni was the key coordinator of the overall exercise.

While we were busy making preparations at the site, we came to know that a private company was drilling nearby for oil. Since our activities also involved drilling of large shafts and boring of tunnels, I wanted to visit the drilling site to understand the technology first-hand. Some of us went there in our army fatigues. While the company engineers were explaining the process, an employee from the company pulled Kulkarni aside, and mentioned that one person in the group looked very much like me. I was, of course, visiting under a different name. Kulkarni naturally denied me being Kakodkar. But the person would not budge. He said that he hailed from Dombivli, a satellite town of Mumbai, and had seen Kakodkar several times. He insisted that I looked very much like Kakodkar. Quietly, Kulkarni whispered into my ears, 'You have been spotted, better scoot.' We wound up the discussion in minutes and bolted.

RACE AGAINST TIME

Everyone got going. The race to meet the deadline turned out to be a photo finish, particularly for the thermonuclear package. Everyone rose to the occasion. The preparations at the site were on a much larger scale compared to 1974. The first set of three tests was carried out on 11 May 1998. They were two high-yield and one low-yield devices. Two days later on 13 May, two lower-yield tests were carried out. The success of the tests was confirmed through near- and far-field seismic measurements, radio chemical measurements, post-test ground movement simulations and other measurements. Apart from proving the fission and thermonuclear weapon capabilities, about a dozen ideas were also validated through further integral tests—the three sub-kiloton tests. India had established the way to build a credible deterrent for the present as well as the future. I believe this was just about the best that was possible within the prevailing constraints.

There was practically no damage to Khetolai. There is an interesting anecdote about the mindset of the villagers. We had to decide the right time to ask them to vacate their houses for the duration of the test as a safety precaution. It was a population of around 5,000, and you could not risk asking them to evacuate too early. At the same time, a minimum time was necessary for the villagers to move out. We asked the army—what was the minimum notice period that was necessary to get the villagers to vacate their houses? They said four hours. When the date and time was finalized, the army personnel went from house to house at the predetermined time and asked them to vacate the village for around seven to eight hours. After the event, at the time of review, we asked the officer (who was a Brigadier) who led the evacuation, about the response of the villagers. He reported that the villagers had been very cooperative. They were aware that some important event was happening, and assured the evacuation team that we need not worry about them. It was a matter of pride for them, and they would stay outside the village for as long as necessary. No one in the village deviated from the plan. It was a revelation that in times of need, people can rise to the occasion, co-operate, and support a national cause. I believe that such sentiments are very important for maintaining national secrets.

Post-test, not too unexpectedly, controversies surfaced about the yield of the tests. Similar incidents had happened after the 1974 test. We had actually released much more evidence about the tests than any other country. Sikka and the seismology group under him did a good job of responding to all issues that were raised. It seemed to me that a good part of the debate was to dig out more details than are normally released. The coupling of the energy of the detonation with the surrounding medium is a crucial factor in the resultant response of the ground and transmission of seismic waves. We decided to demonstrate the significant uncertainties in the yield predictions using seismic records of a hypothetical test. R.K. Singh of BARC developed a code for a 3D simulation of the surrounding medium and the ground surface under the conditions of a nuclear test. This was validated using data from the Baneberry test (carried out in the US in 1970). This validated code was then used to demonstrate the widely varying results that would be obtained in absence of precise knowledge of the surrounding geology. A number of scientific papers were published and contributed in silencing the critics. Singh's code was perhaps the first 3D code of its type. It took a long time to satisfy the referees before the paper was finally published. There was also the issue of the very different surface pattern at the location of the two high-yield tests. The site of the fission weapon test had developed a crater, while that of the thermonuclear test had a mound. This was demonstrated to be entirely consistent with the simulation predictions after accounting for the geology at the two locations.

INTERNATIONAL RAMIFICATIONS

When the tests were being planned, it was expected that after our tests, Pakistan would be compelled to follow suit. Matching India was an existential need for Pakistan. And that did happen on 28 May 1998. There was even a flip-flop in declaring the number of tests, which was reduced to five after an earlier claim pegging them at six. The yield, as assessed by us through detection by our instruments, was much lower than what was announced. Although the statements from Pakistan did confirm that all devices were based on enriched uranium, a third country inferred, on the basis of atmospheric measurements, that plutonium might have been used in a test device. If true, this was a surprise element. It seems that now plutonium production for weapons purposes is going on at an accelerated pace in Pakistan. However, how the plutonium-based weapon designs, which are quite different from uranium weapons, were validated is a mystery—unless they were provided by China.

On 30 May 1998, we were having a relaxed discussion at OYC in the office of Dr Chidambaram. Dr Ramanna and Dr Sikka were also present. During lunch, a thought surfaced that we could expect another Pakistani test, given that it had been two days after their first tests and India had also conducted its second round after a gap of two days. Unsurprisingly, that is what happened. Again, the yield assessed through our measurements was much lower than what was announced.

The Pokhran tests of 1998 gave us a basis for equipping our armed forces with a range of nuclear weapons, ranging from low-yield weapons all the way up to 200 kiloton weapons, all in a range of variants. With the development of nuclear submarine capability, the deterrent truly became a survivable deterrent. With the triad of nuclear weapon launch capability—land, air and sea (including undersea)—having been completed, and having a strong deterrent in place, I believe it is now time to redouble our efforts to redefine and achieve new global and local regimes that assure a more durable all-round peace, in which no one feels insecure. We must realize that while tensions arising out of inequality and the threat they cause to peace are still all around us, the threat of climate change that is knocking on our doors is a much bigger disaster waiting to happen. The only way to address this threat is through the world coming together for a collective global action, where self-interest gives way to collective interest, and everyone acts with the mindset of being a trustee rather than an owner. I hope that wisdom will dawn sooner than later and nuclear weapons will become deterrents that are able to protect peace everywhere around the globe, rather than just being deterrents in the service of national security.

CHAPTER 7

Civil Nuclear Cooperation: Significance beyond the Nuclear Arena

With India arriving on the world scene as a de-facto nuclear weapon state, another national need that was equally important—rapid deployment of nuclear energy—also needed forward traction. While we had realized strategic strength, deployment of nuclear power for clean base load electricity generation needed acceleration. More importantly, looking at the massive energy needs to support India's development and the threat of climate change looming large over the world as a whole, it was clear that rapid growth in nuclear energy deployment was important for both India and the rest of the world. The question was whether one could do something about it.

Around 1998, I was deeply involved with the activities related to the nuclear tests at Pokhran. This included design, fabrication, testing and planning for the tests at the site and elsewhere in the country. This work was primarily being carried out in BARC and a few other laboratories. The philosophy of self-reliant development that had been in place right since Bhabha's time, had enabled the country to take major strides in nuclear technology. Though our atomic energy programme[11] was under international embargo all along, we had maintained uninterrupted progress. The restrictions did not affect the buildup of our strategic capability. In contrast, as mentioned earlier, the nuclear power programme, which has been a much bigger effort, did slow down due to the embargo. But even here, while we were able to master the nuclear technology fully, the setting up of nuclear power plants was affected—initially because of difficulties in procurement of equipment,[12] many of them conventional, and later as a result of shortage of uranium. I recollect an incident related to procurement of an ordinary household item.

We were carrying out decontamination at MAPS at Kalpakkam. Decontamination is a cleaning process wherein the surfaces of components like pipe internals, or general areas having radioactive contamination, are treated with chemical solutions to strip off the contamination. These solutions are then passed through filters and ion exchangers and the radioactive particles are trapped in them. The cleaning circuit designed for MAPS consisted of pipes and valves for circulation of decontaminating solutions. M.K. Nema of RED was coordinating the work at Kalpakkam. He was scouting for valves with smooth finish on the internal surface. If the surface was rough, then the radioactive particles would be lodged in such rough contours. Over time, the particles would accumulate and become hot spots of radiation. Nema found that the conventional fittings used in household bathrooms would fit the bill well and could be used. He

[11]This programme comprises aspects that are beyond nuclear power such as isotope applications, advanced research, etc.

[12]Turbines, pumps, forgings and other equipment are conventional power plant equipment, and as such have no role in nuclear weapon development.

started looking for good-quality bathroom fittings. He located a manufacturer at Karapakkam whose fittings were of good-quality. We went to the company to inspect the components to ensure that they would meet the requirement. The procurement was to be made by MAPS. When we told the company owner that we wanted to buy fittings for use in MAPS, the owner refused to sell. He explained that the manufacturing unit was set up in collaboration with an American firm. As per the agreement with the US firm, the Indian manufacturer was forbidden to sell the products to any Indian nuclear establishment. I was furious with the owner. 'How did you sign an agreement which prevents its sale to an Indian user? Are you not an Indian?' I fumed. Here was a case of embargo on the sale of even ordinary household fittings for use in a nuclear facility—even when they were made in India! We could, of course, move ahead with alternative products in the market, but with some delay. The nuclear power programme faced many such hurdles, and as a result did not progress as fast as we had desired.

It was not as if procurement of components from the open market was completely banned. We did have good experiences as well. In 1985, Dhruva, the research reactor in BARC, was being prepared for its first criticality. Dr Iyengar was keen to have the reactor started at the earliest. The Atomic Energy Regulatory Board (AERB), the regulatory body, imposed a technical condition. In case of loss of primary coolant, there had to be an emergency injection of light water. The primary coolant of Dhruva is heavy water, a commodity as expensive as silver. Spurious ingress of light water in the primary circuit simply could not be allowed. We needed a reliable injection with guaranteed isolation. This was, technically, a contradiction of sorts.

Dr Iyengar went about discussing the problem with anyone he met in BARC. All kind of suggestions were flying thick and fast: Use a diaphragm; or a solenoid plunger arrangement; even a puncture. I told Dr Iyengar that if you punctured it, you would not cut a big hole. And a small hole would not serve the purpose. He then suggested cutting a bigger hole. I explained that in that case, it would need tests and validation, which would easily take four to five months. We were racing against time; counting in terms of weeks. I was irritated and asked him, 'Are you interested in doing something new and innovative or in getting Dhruva on stream quickly?' He, of course, replied that he wanted Dhruva started. I then told him to ignore all suggestions being made and instead use commercially available rupture disks.[13] A company in South India was manufacturing such rupture disks. Two rupture disks could be installed in series, with pressurized space in between for isolation. In case there was need for light water injection, one could simply depressurize this space. This would then cause the outward disc to rupture, and if one disk ruptured then the second would do so as well. The solution was workable, reliable and could be engineered in a short time. Since the rupture disks were commercially available, they could be bought off the shelf. They were procured and successfully installed in the reactor.

Around the same time, in the early '90s, the new amendments to Indian patent law were being worked out. I suggested to the Ministry of Commerce to include a provision that if a product was manufactured in India based on patented technology, then the sale of the product could not be denied to an Indian buyer. The Government of India should have the right to disregard any patent right in case of any such denial. The experts in the Ministry replied that they were engaged in international negotiations and

---

[13]Rupture discs are diaphragms fitted within a pipe that almost instantaneously break once a threshold differential pressure is exceeded, and create a large opening permitting flow to start.

had commitments to honour. They said that to circumvent such problems, there were provisions of compulsory licencing. I studied the compulsory licencing provisions and found that it was a long-drawn process, and was of no practical use. I was agitated with the situation but couldn't do much.

After the 1974 Pokhran PNE experiment, the whole world was against India. Many efforts were made to halt our nuclear programme. Since they could not do that, they started creating hurdles. I gave it deep thought and defined a 'problem statement' for myself. 'How to responsibly make the Non-Proliferation Treaty (NPT) and related international framework irrelevant as far as India's domestic programme is concerned?' India had always maintained that the NPT is discriminatory, and did not sign it. Since by that time many countries had already acceded to the treaty, expecting the NPT to change was out of the question. As Director, BARC, I used to attend the IAEA Board of Governors meetings at Vienna. Every time I went there, I would spend a lot of time with the then Indian Ambassador, Kiran Doshi. I would ask him what the state of world politics would be, five years, ten years, even fifteen years into the future. As a diplomat, he had a better understanding of global dynamics. I would request him to do the crystal gazing and enlighten me. I spent hours understanding the intricacies of diplomacy. I concluded that the way to move forward was to make the world realize that imposing embargoes on India was counterproductive to their own interests. To create this awareness, I thought of many initiatives.

I persuaded S.B. Bhoje, Director, IGCAR, to commence construction of a PFBR at Kalpakkam. The PFBR design had been completed quite some time back. A number of efforts were ongoing to improve things even more. In my view the design work had matured enough, and time was ripe for taking up construction. Delay in such a decision could, in my view, have consequences in terms of the fading of political support. I had, in fact, received hints to that effect from responsible senior politicians. A bold decision was therefore necessary. When you begin construction of such a fast reactor, you also have to be ready to supply tonne quantities of plutonium inventory to operate it. While initiating the second stage of India's nuclear power programme (eventually achieved in 2004) was of course an important milestone in itself, it could also convey a strong message about the county's strategic depth and readiness because of the sizeable quantity of plutonium involved. To drive the message home, I invited the Prime Minister, Dr Manmohan Singh, for the ceremonial first pour of concrete at Kalpakkam. Traditionally in DAE, a dignitary like the Prime Minister only makes visits to dedicate a completed facility to the nation, and not for the first pour of concrete. Dr Singh's speech on the occasion was targeted at the international audience, and it had the desired impact.

GLOBAL POLICY SHIFT

Every year, IAEA conducts its General Conference around September. It is an event attended by ministers and senior officials of almost all the member states. A slot is allotted for all member states to address the conference in the form of a national statement. The national statement highlights their respective national positions in the context of prevailing global dynamics, suggestions for specific IAEA actions, and major achievements of the countries in the field of atomic energy. I saw a major opportunity in this and started including our developments of strategic significance in my speeches. For example, in my statement at the General Conference, I once spoke of laser enrichment, which is a sensitive topic. Normally we do not talk of such topics in public forums. Such deliberate inclusions were not flashy but instead, over a period of three to four years, gradually built up the image of India's strategic capability.

Every year, during the General Conference at Vienna, the Chinese would hold a reception in a restaurant close to the IAEA headquarters. The leader of the Chinese delegation, my counterpart, would appear very friendly and smile a lot, but keep mum. I narrated this to Shiv Shankar Menon, who was the Indian Ambassador in Beijing at that time (2000-03). I asked him what he thought of such gestures. Menon told me not to ignore them; 'They want to be friends with you but won't admit it.' I followed that advice and developed a rapport with my Chinese counterpart.

We needed low-enriched uranium (LEU) fuel for our reactors TAPS 1 and 2. China had once supplied this in the past. I asked him to do so again. He replied that they were short of uranium and no longer in a position to supply. By 2004, we reached a level to be able to start talking about possibilities for soft cooperation. Both countries were setting up Russian pressurized water reactors, commonly known as VVERs, and both had PHWRs. China was interested in fast reactors, and India was way ahead in fast reactor technology. India had an interest in high-temperature reactors, where China was ahead of us. There was a perfect balance for give and take. The soft cooperation could manifest in the form of occasional seminars or meetings. One could retract any time if conditions so demanded. Once at Vienna, the Chinese shared their concern on the VVER steam generators that had been supplied to them. They told us that the steam generators had developed cracks. We too were importing such steam generators from Russia for Kudankulam and the Chinese wanted us to be careful. S.K. Jain, then CMD of NPCIL, was with me. He responded that we were well aware of such a possibility. NPCIL did not face such problems as it had already set up a detailed protocol for packaging and transport. The mutual interest thus grew. The Chinese invited us to visit them. It was decided that I should lead a delegation to China that included, among others, Jain and Srikumar Banerjee, Director, BARC. We did visit China in 2005. While the visit was on, I was asked to return to join the delegation to be led by the PM to the United States. There was no question of any further progress on the Chinese front, at least for the foreseeable future.

CEMENTING A STRATEGIC PARTNERSHIP

Post the 1998 tests, exhaustive engagement between India and the US began in the form of the Jaswant Singh–Strobe Talbot dialogue. Around 2001, when Bush became President of United States, US Ambassador Robert Blackwell and Ashley Tellis started discussing the wider geo-politics and India's role in it. This placed the emerging India in an important position, especially as a counter to China. Sustained engagement with Americans along with prevailing dynamics in various quarters led to Americans coming up with a proposal for the 'Next Steps in Strategic Partnership' (NSSP) with India that was formally announced in January 2004. The domains covered were atomic energy, space, high-technology trade and missile defence. There were some useful proposals with respect to space and defence, but there was little in terms of atomic energy. The seeds of the Indo-US defence cooperation, however, were sown in this initiative. Brajesh Mishra, the then National Security Advisor (NSA), had asked me for my opinion. 'This proposal has come from the US, what we should do about this? If you are interested, then only we will go ahead.' I replied that, per se, there was nothing significant in the proposal for atomic energy. But the optics looked good and

I was game about going ahead with it.

NSSP had well-defined goals, to be mutually realized in different steps. Things, however, moved very fast. Several things literally collapsed into each other. NSSP, which was announced in January 2004, was declared as an action completed successfully in July 2005. Clearly the iron was hot, ready for the strike.

Meanwhile another international joint-initiative was taking shape: The International Thermonuclear Experimental Reactor (ITER) for fusion research. Around 2003-05, the members of ITER were China, European Union (EU), Japan, Russia, Republic of Korea and USA. A tussle was going on with respect to the site for ITER. The Japanese wanted it on their soil and the EU was pressing for Cadarache in France. The two sides were evenly matched. Each time I was in Vienna, the French would seek me out and ask India to join ITER. French President Jacques Chirac had also written to Prime Minister Vajpayee, requesting India to join ITER. Initially, I didn't pay much heed to this, as it meant spending large sums of money. Although very important from a long-term perspective, we had other programmes with higher priority. When Brajesh Mishra asked for my take on the French proposal, I told him that while fusion energy was very important in the long term, and India's stature, globally, would grow considerably on joining ITER, doing so would cost a lot. He said that India had limited resources and did not have the luxury to invest just for prestige. The proposal was put in cold storage. The French were persistent in following it up, but our view remained unchanged. However, around the time the NSSP was taking shape and other initiatives started warming up, I indicated to Brajesh Mishra, 'Now is the time to move forward on ITER'.

During my next visit to IAEA, in September 2004, I enquired with the European members of ITER about the process of joining it, and the steps India should take to move forward. Following this, I invited a group from the EU to visit the Institute for Plasma Research (IPR) in Gandhinagar, where most of the fusion energy research was taking place. The visit took place promptly in November 2004. After the visit, the team halted in Mumbai on their way back. I distinctly remember that it was Deepawali day. I met the group in a hotel near the airport. They were driving hard for India to join ITER.

Within a few days of the visit, they completed the formality of concluding that India was qualified to join ITER. They also advised us to formally contact all members of ITER. I reported this to the Prime Minister's Office (PMO), under Dr Manmohan Singh, suggesting that we now needed to mount a diplomatic effort with all ITER member countries. MEA did a good job and succeeded in garnering support. Communications were sent to all these countries and followed up by our embassies there. Initially there was some reluctance on part of the Japanese. This was perhaps because of aforementioned negotiations related to the site of the ITER, which got sorted out eventually. I received a message from a senior member of Japanese parliament (who used to be a minister earlier), requesting for a meeting. The day he proposed for the meeting was a holiday. I offered to meet him in Khyber, a restaurant in south Mumbai. He arrived in the morning in Delhi, took the first flight to Mumbai, met me in the restaurant over lunch, returned to Delhi, and took the flight back to Tokyo on the same day. He had come to convey that if India felt that Japan had been negative in its approach towards India joining ITER, then that was not true. He had travelled all the way from Tokyo to Mumbai just to deliver this message. I was quite struck by the nuanced Japanese approach.

Our relations with Russia were special, with deep strategic significance. After the 1998 tests, although there were serious constraints because of the respective political positions of India and Russia, as well as respective international and domestic legal commitments, Russia did pursue ways to cooperate on the Kudankulam 1 and 2 project. This could work out since there was already an old agreement on this, inked during the Soviet era, that could be grandfathered. Soon after the 1998 tests, Yevgeny Adamov, the then Chief of the Russian Ministry for Atomic Energy (MINATOM) had visited BARC. Informally, he congratulated us for the tests. He said that Russia was with India but could not support us openly. He proposed to move forward on additional VVER reactors. In fact, in October 2000, President Vladimir Putin visited India, during which a declaration on Strategic Partnership was signed and the mechanism of the annual Summit-level interaction was reiterated. I was informed by the Russian side that President Putin would visit BARC during this trip and would want to be photographed with Dhruva in the background. I relayed this to MEA, who had no information on this matter till then. He did come to BARC and got himself photographed. The photograph was immediately flashed across global media. I thought this gesture during his first visit after 1998 Pokhran tests to be very significant.

France had also reacted similarly. In 1985, we were negotiating a light water reactor with them. That was before France joined NPT. They too congratulated us informally after the 1998 tests and expressed serious interest in exploring ways for further cooperation in the area of nuclear power a little later. However, while both Russia and France were keen on developing nuclear power business with India, they were clear that dialogue with the Americans to bring them on board was a prerequisite for any meaningful way forward. They could not move forward unless the Americans were on board. They both were bound by their respective obligations under the NSG. The only way forward was an NSG exemption for India. Both these countries along with the USA played a key role in mobilizing global opinion in favour of creating an NSG exemption for India.

The key arguments for such a major global policy shift were based on a) the geo-politics prevailing then, which favoured mainstreaming India, b) growing energy needs in India, with the threat of climate change in case they were primarily met by fossil sources, c) the large market opportunity for nuclear power in India, d) recognition of India's track record as a responsible country with advanced nuclear technology and e) stability of the global hydrocarbon market in light of perceived large growth in demand in India (Shale oil/gas was yet to become big at that time).

A HUGE TECTONIC SHIFT

In 2005, when it was time for me to lead a delegation to China, I knew that Prime Minister Dr Manmohan Singh was scheduled to visit Washington. From messages that were being exchanged around, I had sensed that something related to nuclear would come up during the visit. Sure enough, while I was in Beijing, I received a call from New Delhi asking me to return. Dr Singh wanted me to travel with him to Washington. Our delegation was to stay in Beijing for a few more days and then proceed to Vietnam. I handed over the reins to Dr Banerjee and rushed back to New Delhi, and I accompanied Dr Singh on his aircraft to Washington.

Before the visit, numerous messages containing a variety of proposals and formulations were flying back and forth. This continued even as we were flying on way to Washington. MEA was clearly on overdrive. India and USA seeking to develop civil nuclear cooperation was a huge tectonic shift in international

A young Anil Kakodkar with his mother, Kamala Kakodkar.

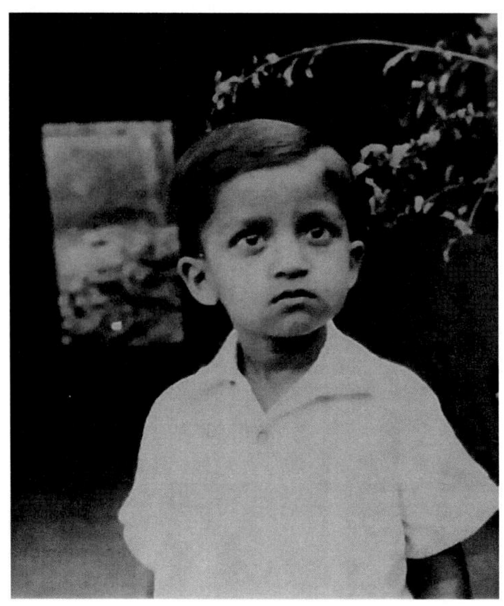

As a young student.

Graduating in Engineering from Bombay University.

As a member of a delegation to Russia in 1981.

Dr Kakodkar (third from left) along with Suresh Gangotra (centre) at the graduation dinner of the twenty-seventh Batch of the BARC Training School (1984).

At Pokhran with the team in 1998.

At Pokhran with Prime Minister A.B. Vajpayee and the team.

Dr Kakodkar with Russian President Vladimir Putin and Dr R. Chidambaram. The Research Reactor Dhruva in the background. October 2000.

Shaking hands with US President George Bush.

With Prime Minister Dr Manmohan Singh and other dignitaries on the occasion of dedicating Tarapur Atomic Power Station units 3 & 4 to the nation.

President Jacques Chirac and President Barroso with signatories of the ITER Agreement, Elysée Palace, Paris, 21 November 2006.

Signing of the Indo-French Agreement for nuclear cooperation in Paris, in the presence of France's President, Nicolas Sarkozy, and India's then Prime Minister Dr Manmohan Singh.

Inspecting a nuclear power plant.

Meeting the Director General of IAEA, Dr Mohamed ElBaradei.

Addressing the General Conference of IAEA at Vienna.

Engaging with the Indian media.

Dr Kakodkar with Yukiya Amano, former DG of IAEA.

Dr Kakodkar leaving the office of Secretary, DAE on 30 November 2009.

Chairmen of Atomic Energy Commission (L to R): Dr R. Chidambaram, Dr P.K. Iyengar, Dr M.R. Srinivasan, Dr Anil Kakodkar and Dr Raja Ramanna.

Dr Kakodkar with mother, wife, daughters, sons-in-law and grandchildren.

Dr Kakodkar with sister, wife and daughters.

Dr Kakodkar, accompanied by mother, wife and sister, receiving Goa's highest civilian award, the Gomantak Vibhushan award.

Receiving the Padma Vibhushan from President Pratibha Devi Singh Patil.

politics. This was in complete contrast with the decades of efforts to deny any nuclear commerce to India through a global non-proliferation architecture that was painstakingly created post India's 1974 PNE experiment, as discussed before. The euphoria at one stage appeared to create an impression that the 'nuclear weapon state' status for India was around the corner. There were, however, several serious pitfalls in the formulations that were being floated. Thus, even though I was in favour of developing this cooperation from an energy perspective, I was more concerned with preserving and ensuring protection of India's strategic autonomy, which was under serious threat. The issue of strategic autonomy was crucial for both our weapons programme and sustained development of our three-stage nuclear programme. I was carefully looking at every word in the proposed formulations from this perspective. Ironically, thus, I myself had to apply brakes on what I had been patiently working on for many years as there could be no compromise on our strategic autonomy. There was a section that felt that this was a lifetime opportunity for India that should not be missed at any cost. I thus began to look like a villain, coming in the way of a great deal for many in both countries. We had defined red lines that nobody could be allowed to cross. Colleagues from the PMO, specially Sujata Mehta and Venkatesh Varma, were a great help and support all through these negotiations. Internally, I was convinced that the Americans needed us much more than we needed them, and that the deal would go through.

On reaching Washington the evening of the day before the summit, there was an internal meeting at the hotel we were staying in to take stock of the state of play till that time. Among those present were Dr Singh, Foreign Minister Natwar Singh, Minister of State Prithvi Raj Chavan, NSA M.K. Narayanan, Foreign Secretary Shyam Saran, Ambassador Ronen Sen and other members from PMO and MEA. The draft statement as it existed till that time was being discussed. There was a strong opinion that this was an important and historic opportunity and we should not let it go. The Prime Minister sought everybody's opinion. Everyone was either in strong or cautious support. I was the last to be asked.

When my turn came, I had to bring out inherent risks. I explained that we couldn't open up cooperation in certain areas of the nuclear programme that impacted our strategic programme as well as the evolving three-stage programme, and risk their becoming vulnerable to external constraints. Such programmes had to be completely insulated. We could accept cooperation for facilities, which we could place under IAEA safeguards with the assurance of uninterrupted lifetime supplies. Our experience with Tarapur had to be kept in view and adequate safeguards ensured. As the formulation on the table did not meet these expectations, I did not support the text and expressed the need for further changes to make it satisfactory from our point of view. I was in favour of the cooperation but the proposed draft was not acceptable.

The moment I said that, several seniors pounced upon me. 'Atomic energy is not the only concern; you have to think about the country.' Finally, the PM said, 'If Kakodkar says no, then we can't go ahead.' I remember Natwar Singh reprimanding me right in front of the PM. Ronen Sen (who was in DAE for a short while a long time back, and was closely involved with several nuclear diplomatic engagements in the past) began talking like an expert in atomic energy and tried to negate my serious reservations. I was being singled out as the fall guy. All this was very painful.

However, diplomats on both sides continued working through the night to make the text mutually acceptable. The next morning, even as the formal programme was about to start, I was called by the PM. Natwar Singh was also present. The text was still not acceptable. Natwar Singh then asked me to write down the formulation that would be acceptable. I scribbled it on a paper napkin lying on the table. He took the paper, folded it, put it in his pocket and went for the meeting. Things were going down to the wire. At lunch, MEA officials showed me the latest draft. The text was now acceptable and I said so. After the draft was finalized, news broke out about the Joint Statement.

With the job done, the delegation was to return to Delhi. I wanted to fly back directly to Mumbai. I went to see Dr Manmohan Singh and take leave. Dr Singh, visibly relieved, said, 'Yesterday night I couldn't sleep. I stayed awake, praying throughout. You have saved the country.' I naturally felt very comforted given the onslaught that I had suffered. It was clear that implementation of all elements embedded in the Joint Statement could happen only on the basis of treating India like a nuclear weapon state, even though nobody would say so explicitly. This was a tectonic shift. Consequently, there were major challenges ahead—both nationally and internationally.

ACCOMMODATING THE NEW REALITY

The next step was the matter of detailing engagements, in the backdrop of these challenges, not only with US but also with other key countries as well as multilateral bodies like IAEA, Nuclear Supplier's Group (NSG), and others. This was critical, as the devil could lie in the details. We had already created a Strategic Planning Group in DAE under R.B. Grover. Representation of MEA in the external relations wing of DAE had also been upgraded from deputy secretary level to joint secretary level. The group had prepared well to deal with the detailed negotiations to follow. There were several elements to deal with: agreements with the US and several other countries, India's Separation Plan that delineates civilian and military facilities, India Specific Safeguards Agreement with IAEA, revisiting several multilateral arrangements from India's perspective and so on.

Soon the tussle started. Negotiations with the US were the toughest. They spanned a wide range of issues covering different actions envisaged in the Joint Statement. Aligning the new expectations and the legal framework of both countries was a major challenge. On the US side, the prevailing framework had deep connotations of the post-1974 non-proliferation web that has been created. Changing that to accommodate the new reality in the backdrop of the political environment that existed was a challenge. There could also be an underlying current of leveraging new arrangements to maximize control on the Indian programme.

On the Indian side, the challenge was to insulate the strategic programme as well as the emerging development activities from any external control. Further, there was this aspect of protecting the assets within the purview of cooperation, should the cooperation breakdown for some reason. We had the experience of Tarapur units 1 and 2 suffering following the 1974 PNE experiment. Here we were talking of a much bigger engagement, and so the risks were bigger. A diverse and multilayered sourcing arrangement, especially for uranium, had to be ensured. All this was to be consistent with the national foreign policy related to nuclear issues.

It was Narayanan's idea that the two of us would not sit on the negotiating table but be constantly available for guidance. This allowed us to do somewhat relaxed reflection on the proceedings that were taking place and carry out any mid-course corrections that might be necessary. The primary interlocutors were Shyam Saran and Nicholas Burns. Whenever it was needed, the two

NSAs, Narayanan and Stephen Hadley, met. R.B. Grover and the Joint Secretary, ER, would represent DAE in the negotiations. Once, when in Washington for negotiations, Narayanan and I stayed back in our rooms in the hotel while the negotiations were in progress. Every two or three hours, a new draft would arrive, and we would all meet to discuss it. It was a long-drawn battle but the strategy was very useful in making our negotiations robust.

Developing the Separation Plan needed deep and careful thinking. It had to be ensured that the decision of what was civil and what was military would remain exclusively an Indian decision, in the present and the future. The capacity factor of the nuclear reactors was continuously going down due to uranium supply not being able to cope up with the increasing needs. Various strategies to augment domestic uranium production had already been put in place. Similarly, significant investment in terms of technology and financial resources for augmented exploration of uranium were also made. All this was sure to enable a significantly larger availability of indigenous uranium for the reactors in due course of time (this has indeed happened, with our uranium resource potential now being three-times larger). PHWR technology had well-matured by then and running parallel streams, one outside IAEA safeguards and another under IAEA safeguards, was entirely feasible, even after accounting for the fact that spent fuel management and recycling for reactors under IAEA safeguards would need dedicated reprocessing and fuel re-fabrication facilities. We had already been pursuing the policy of accepting IAEA safeguards for reactors running on external inputs right since the Tarapur days. So, as long as the fuel supply could be assured, we would be consistent with existing policies while adopting such an approach. One could thus also envisage a much bigger PHWR programme as compared to the 10,000 MWe capacity that was visualized early on. Looking at the needs of our strategic and three-stage programme development as well as the current uranium supply position, one had to decide on the number of reactors that should be kept outside IAEA safeguards. With this approach, one could quickly ramp up the capacity factor of our reactors and ensure the financial health of NPCIL. Keeping all these in mind, the contours of the Separation Plan were worked out.

Tarapur 1 and 2 and Kudankulam 1 and 2 were already under IAEA safeguards, as they were imported reactors. Rajasthan 1 and 2 reactors were built with Canadian cooperation and so they were also under IAEA safeguards. We decided to offer eight more 220 MWe PHWRs (total capacity 1760 MWe) for IAEA safeguards, thus taking the total number of reactors to be placed under IAEA safeguards to fourteen. Along with this, the 540 MWe Tarapur units 3 & 4 and six more 220 MWe PHWRs at Kaiga and Kalpakkam—totalling a capacity of 2400 MWe—remained outside IAEA safeguards. The fast reactor and thorium programme, including the related fuel cycle programme, was kept outside IAEA safeguards in its entirety. Apart from the details of Separation Plan, several other measures to protect against potential disruption of supplies to reactors under IAEA safeguards also had to be incorporated. Since we had already suffered with Tarapur 1 and 2, we had to be extra careful. Layered measures incorporating a number of diverse and redundant arrangements were built in. Building a uranium stock pile to meet lifetime requirements of reactors under IAEA safeguards was one such important measure. While these numbers for reactors and provisions for assured fuel supply were arrived at with a very careful consideration of several aspects, getting them accepted, even internally, was a challenge. Particularly, the aspect of strategic stockpiling sufficient to meet lifetime requirements was crucial, as significant capital would get locked up in this process.

The Prime Minister showed considerable foresight and statesmanship in taking such a decision. Getting Americans to accept the Separation Plan and related provisions was an even bigger task. I was however, clear in my mind that we were negotiating from a position of strength and the proposal would go through. As expected, things went down to the wire once again and the negotiations were still on even as it was time for President Bush to arrive in New Delhi in March 2006 for the next bilateral summit, just around nine months after the Washington Joint Statement.

When the negotiations were passing through rough weather due to differences on contours of the Separation Plan, I was amused with the name-calling that happened during that time. The bone of contention was reprocessing—whether to include or exclude it. The US-India Business Council (USIBC) was among other lobbies pushing for the early finalization of the cooperation agreement. They were driven by industry interests on both sides. In Delhi, they would lobby with higher echelons in MEA, the Planning Commission, the PMO, the Ministry of Commerce and others. Once or twice they did want to meet me, but I maintained a safe distance from them. After a few rounds of visits to India, they probably came to the conclusion that they must meet me.

During their next visit they were insistent on meeting me. We finally agreed for a short meeting at Hotel Taj, just a stone's throw from the DAE office in Mumbai. The leader of the Council delegation, Ron Somers, in his introductory remarks mentioned that they had been wanting to talk to me for a long time. Everybody in New Delhi seemed to be fine with the elements of the agreement, but the only hurdle was Anil Kakodkar.

They were unable to understand why I was taking a negative stand on demands that were being made for inclusion in the Separation Plan. I requested for a five minute-long uninterrupted intervention. I told them that it was my responsibility to develop and steer the atomic energy programme in India. PHWR development was not the end of that mission. It was the beginning. There were many more new technologies, not existing anywhere, particularly in the context of our long-term interests in thorium, that had to be developed. I could not be doing that with the IAEA inspectors breathing down my neck. When we were doing something new, we would naturally need mid-course corrections. Something would work. Something would not. If we were under IAEA safeguards and made even a small deviation, we would be accused of doing something that was not in the agreed plan. R&D can never be done like that. We had the second stage and the third stage of the programme to work on. Reprocessing and enrichment were integral to this mission. All these were fundamental to the progress of nuclear energy in India. I then asked him whether he agreed with what I said and offered to respond to further queries. He admitted that what I had said appeared logical. I then told him that if they understood, then rather than wasting their time here in India, they should do the talking in Washington to get things sorted out. The next I heard about USIBC was a news item emanating in the US suggesting that the problem with the US-India dialogue was that there was a 600-pound gorilla in the room by the name of Anil Kakodkar, who talked logic but wouldn't budge. When someone asked me about my being branded a 600-pound gorilla, I only said, 'I take it as a compliment'. USIBC in 2009 graciously recognized me with the USIBC Award for Expansion of US-India Trade Relations.

Two days prior to the President's arrival, the US team was in New Delhi to finalize the text of the Separation Plan. We were negotiating in South Block right till 2:00 AM on the night before President Bush was to arrive. Firmness paid off. The US team conceded to our demands. The next morning, there was the formal meeting at Hyderabad House. By that time, I was already being perceived as a difficult nut to crack. When I was introduced to President Bush, he asked, 'So, you are that Kakodkar. Are you happy?' I replied in the affirmative. The next step was to further detail out the Agreements.

While all this was happening, there was another challenge to face. Media was full of stories about negotiations, coming from a variety of quarters. Some, it seemed to me, were even planted stories. I was increasingly being perceived as a spoiler of a potentially important opportunity for India. *The Indian Express* in one of its editorials even questioned whether DAE was functioning under Government of India or not.

I decided to clear my stand and did an interview with Pallava Bagla. The next day it appeared in *Indian Express* (8 February 2006), almost a full-page article. A photograph of mine against the backdrop of India Gate at New Delhi was also included. The interview enabled me to present a perspective of the DAE and a rationale for the tough path of negotiations that we were pursuing. It spelt out the red lines and why it was in India's interests to adhere to them without any compromise. I started looking almost like a rebel. Though I knew I had the backing of the PM, I was aware that the government was not a monolith. There were divergent views within the government. I had to put my foot down and that was the reason I went public with my stand. While doing so, I had kept my resignation letter in my pocket and was ready to put in the papers if the situation so demanded.

The interview did have the desired effect. The people pulled back, realizing that Kakodkar meant business and wouldn't budge. I must also say that the PM's support was crucial during all this. He, at one stage, even made a public statement that the government policy on atomic energy was what the DAE recommended. Within MEA itself, there was a divide on the issue. I had sympathizers and supporters in MEA who would urge me to be careful and firm. There was a faction that understood the nuances. They may not have understood the technical aspects fully but they did understand the dynamics extremely well. Through them I would also receive the next day's news in advance.

Global events also worked in our favour. I had heard President Bush expressing that growth of nuclear power in India was in the US interest, to take the pressure off the global demand for energy, and to that end it would help the American consumer by keeping a check on oil prices.[14] The US had not yet seen large-scale commercialization of shale oil and shale gas by then. Long-term price of petroleum was a concern and US did not want a country like India to be an oil guzzler as her economy grew. The atmosphere for nuclear cooperation had become relatively favourable in the US.

I was keen on not leaving any open-ended issues before I left office. Leaving open-ended issues could pose a risk in terms of things drifting towards undesirable consequences. Considering the complexities involved, the negotiations could have gone on for years or more than a decade. When they linger for too long, you do not know what turn of events in the future would affect the contours of cooperation. Luckily, the finalization of the Agreement was relatively swift.

While all this was happening, significant unease was building up among the elders within the DAE community. Homi Sethna, P.K. Iyengar, A.N. Prasad (former Director, BARC) and

---

[14]'But the other thing that our Congress has got to understand is that it's in our economic interests that India have a civilian nuclear power industry to help take the pressure off the global demand for energy,' the President said. 'To the extent that we can reduce demand for fossil fuels, it will help the American consumer.' CBS News, 28 February 2006

A. Gopalakrishnan (former Chairman, AERB) began raising a hue and cry against the nuclear deal in public. I had a meeting with them to explain the need for opening up of civil nuclear cooperation, the current technological depth of the programme to be able to deal with contingencies, measures to insulate strategic- and future-development programmes to enable self-reliant progress, and the precautions being built in to tide over potential disruptions. I felt that they were convinced of the approach. But perhaps the distrust and the fear about such a major transition was too high, and things were back to square one the very next day.

It was then that I decided to set up their meeting with the PM. The meeting took place in August 2006 in Delhi. Sethna had dealt with Americans post 1974. He had the bitter experience of dealing with them with respect to supply of fuel for TAPS 1 and 2. He was of the firm opinion that the Americans could not be trusted. It was explained that we were alert to all such apprehensions and the experience of the past was being leveraged in shaping the new deal. Apart from my proximity to Sethna, he and Dr Singh also had a good rapport. When Sethna was Chairman, AEC, Dr Manmohan Singh was the Finance Secretary and a member of AEC. Sethna came on board but others continued their tirade against the nuclear deal. Though all of them were retired, their opinion could affect the morale of the working community within DAE. It became a challenge to remain engaged with the larger community as well as the opinion makers within the government and the general public, and explain how a deal done on our terms would be advantageous to us. Luckily, the support from such broader stakeholder bases such as colleagues within DAE, industry, and the broader scientific community was indeed overwhelming. More importantly, the working community within DAE was confident and saw a major opportunity.

Securing NSG waiver for India was a part of the understanding reached with the US. Russia and France had earlier expressed the need to secure such an exemption to start dealing with India in terms of nuclear commerce. Surely, they must have worked behind the scenes with USA and others to lobby for the Indian case. By this time, Shiv Shankar Menon had become Foreign Secretary. Earlier, Menon had done a stint in DAE when Ramanna was Chairman. I had known him since then. Diplomatic activity on the part of India, the US and a few other countries became intense, to seek a clean NSG waiver for India. In a conversation with Menon around this period, we even toyed with the idea of seeking NSG membership itself. This, however, did not get pursued. The negotiations for NSG exemption were tough and Menon did an excellent job and secured the clean waiver for India.

Another equally important step to be realized concurrently was to develop an India Specific Safeguards Agreement (ISSA) between India and IAEA. Generally, there are three kinds of safeguards agreements that IAEA has with the member states. One is the comprehensive safeguards agreement that brings all nuclear facilities and material in a country under the purview of IAEA safeguards. All non-nuclear weapon states under the NPT are covered by such a safeguard agreement. The second is the facility specific agreement that applies only to a specific facility for which a member state has requested safeguard coverage. The third is the voluntary offer agreement that is meant for the nuclear weapons states under the NPT and covers only those facilities that are voluntarily offered by the member state for application of IAEA safeguards. Under the new arrangement, India was to voluntarily offer some of her facilities for application of IAEA safeguards. In that sense our agreement with IAEA had to change from the second type to the third type. India was also placing some of her facilities under IAEA safeguards voluntarily. So, the text of the ISSA had to be modelled on the lines of the voluntary safeguards agreement used by nuclear weapon states.

Dr El Baradei, then Director General of IAEA, was a good friend. He agreed that what we were saying was legally correct. He also guided us and the IAEA staff in developing the agreement. IAEA being a multilateral organization, where the ultimate approval is in the hands of the Board of Governors and the Member States, steering such an out-of-the-box agreement could be full of complexities. Thankfully, we were successful in getting the ISSA finalized in a short time. We now actually have an ISSA like those of nuclear weapons states, duly approved by the IAEA.

NSG waiver, ISSA and internal legislative processes in key countries paved the way for signing the bilateral cooperation agreement with USA, France and Russia, followed by other countries. A lot of prior ground work was already done and so these agreements came into existence rather quickly after NSG waiver and ISSA.

TOWARDS A BROADER LIABILITY FRAMEWORK

One task I could not accomplish during my tenure was the finalization of the Civil Liability Nuclear Damage (CLND) Act. The need for such a legislation was recognized way earlier than the beginning of discussion on civil nuclear cooperation. Study groups had done detailed work and had worked out the necessary details. However, having started the discussions on civil nuclear cooperation, it was necessary to await the final shape of things. Around the time the bill came up for discussion in mid-2010, the court verdict on the Bhopal Gas Tragedy came in. This charged the public discourse on the nuclear liability issue and brought in more onerous provisions for supplier liability well beyond the framework prevailent internationally.

I personally believe that the Indian innovation, in principle, would be a significant improvement to the international liability regime. The future is likely to see a much larger growth in supply of nuclear plants by developed countries to developing countries, and broader supplier liability framework is indeed necessary. However, the way it happened was rather impractical, very disruptive and without sufficient stakeholder engagement. Industry stopped bidding even for ongoing domestic projects. Tenders for several key components of the Gorakhpur Power Project in Haryana—a new project that had just been launched—did not find any takers. This also became an additional hurdle in picking up momentum for the projects to be set up through international cooperation. A lot of time was lost in getting the industry to understand the implications of the Act. It was only after a much-delayed formal articulation on how the supplier liability is to be interpreted and establishment of an appropriate insurance product, that things seemed to be getting back on track. Clearly, we might have lost several years of programme progress in the process.

I feel sad when I look back at the progress made consequent to opening up of international cooperation in nuclear energy. By 2010, almost all agreements and instruments for cooperation were in place. If the ongoing construction of PHWRs had continued uninterrupted, and the construction of projects with foreign collaboration had commenced between 2010 and 2012, significant capacity addition with PHWRs could have taken place and at least one reactor set up with international cooperation would have been ready for commissioning by now. The initiative for construction of ten PHWR units of domestic design in fleet mode is indeed a welcome sign. The VVER programme with Russian cooperation also seems to have taken off well.

Westinghouse and Areva, the two other vendors, seemed to have their own troubles in the meantime, causing delays in taking up these projects. Westinghouse had its own financial troubles and had to go through bankruptcy proceedings. The French government redefined the scope of Areva, and responsibility for the Jaitapur project got transferred to Électricité de France (EDF) from Areva. Our PHWRs have an important purpose of serving as a benchmark for judging economic competitiveness of proposals by foreign vendors. The work content in a Light Water Reactor (LWR), the kind of reactors being marketed by foreign vendors, is actually lower than a PHWR. As such, the capital cost of LWR should, in principle, be about 25 per cent lower. In reality, it is the other way around. The reason is primarily the cost difference between manufacture in India vis-à-vis manufacture in richer economies with higher cost of living.

It is for this reason that I have, from the beginning, emphasized domestic manufacture even for reactors supplied by foreign vendors. I wish that we make rapid progress in this regard and make India a manufacturing hub for nuclear equipment for domestic as well as foreign markets. We should see several joint ventures between foreign technology holders and domestic industry, which I believe would be a win-win situation for both. These ventures would make foreign players more competitive and would push the technological capability of Indian players. Also, the tariff for electricity generated in these plants would be lower, alongside much greater high-tech industrial manufacturing activity in the country. Several imaginative and proactive steps are of course necessary. I do believe that nuclear share in the overall energy supply must get ramped up rapidly to combat the climate change crisis. Renewables are of course important, but without nuclear, which is the only possible non-fossil base load source in the grid, the challenge is unlikely to be met.

The story of international cooperation in nuclear energy is incomplete without mentioning the Global Centre for Nuclear Energy Partnership (GCNEP) at Bahadurgarh in Haryana. It all started with the activities of the Nuclear Threat Initiative (NTI), a US-based think tank. NTI was working on two fronts—the IAEA and the US government. A dedicated nuclear security programme was initiated at IAEA, which had significant funding from NTI. Nuclear security, while very important, was a sensitive subject and collaborative programmes had to be dealt with carefully. I had articulated that we would be happy with organizing multilateral programmes under the IAEA banner, particularly for the developing countries. However, there were also instances when a meeting between IAEA and India would be proposed. Once the details were worked out, it would turn out to be essentially a bilateral engagement. I then had to play blow hot-blow cold. We held all such meetings at Vashi, a satellite township of Mumbai, but never allowed them to visit BARC. The programme was going well and earned India a lot of goodwill.

Around 2009, the international nuclear security discourse started receiving much greater importance and attention. The idea to organize a Nuclear Security Summit biannually got crystallized. The first such summit took place in early 2010. The US had also proposed a government-to-government bilateral programme relating to nuclear security. It was at this time that I proposed that we should set up a separate international centre somewhere closer to Delhi to promote all such activities and more, covering all aspects of atomic energy. This was proposed as a response to the US proposal when Narayanan and I had visited the country for a meeting with his counterpart in 2009. Everybody was happy with the proposal. I am happy that the Centre has now taken shape.

The opening of International Civil Nuclear Cooperation for India has significance far beyond the nuclear arena. It has brought

India into the mainstream, fairly close to the position that she deserves. It has opened doors for access to high technology in a wide variety of sectors. Most importantly, India can now be a more effective player in geopolitics for her own benefit as well as for the rest of the world. Apart from access to uranium and cooperation with Russia, we can still expect growth in cooperation with the US (at least with Westinghouse) and France. I believe we can steer the cooperation beyond just the vendor-buyer relationship with big nuclear companies. There are several high-potential engagements possible between the industries on both sides. Through such engagements one could explore markets in the developing world where the need for additional nuclear energy is, in my view, the maximum. We can leverage India's vast thorium resources to enable growth of nuclear energy worldwide without the fear of nuclear proliferation. This, in fact, is the need of the hour in light of the climate change threat that the world is facing.

NOTE ON THE THREE-STAGE NUCLEAR POWER PROGRAMME

FISSILE & FERTILE NUCLEI

A nucleus (like U-235) that can undergo fission is called a fissile nucleus. U-235 is the only naturally occurring fissile isotope. The natural uranium contains only about 0.7 per cent of the fissile U-235. The rest of it, i.e. 99.3 per cent, is the other isotope with atomic mass 238 (U-238). When bombarded with neutrons, rather than undergoing fission, it absorbs the neutron and transforms into another nucleus i.e. plutonium-239 (with atomic number 94 and atomic mass 239). Plutonium-239 can undergo fission like U-235. A nucleus like U-238, which does not itself undergo fission but can give birth to another fissile nucleus, is called a fertile nucleus. Thorium (atomic number 92 and atomic mass 232), which is found abundantly in India, is also a fertile nucleus and when bombarded with neutron gives birth to another fissile isotope of uranium i.e. U-233.

THE THREE-STAGE INDIAN NUCLEAR POWER PROGRAMME

India has a unique three-stage nuclear power programme designed to make use of the modest uranium resources and abundant thorium resources in the country. The salient feature of the programme is that the first stage provides fuel for the second stage and that in turn provides the fuel for the third stage.

In the first stage, U-235 (either as natural or enriched uranium) is used as the fissile material. The indigenous PHWRS use natural uranium, and the two Boiling Water Reactors (TAPS 1 and 2) and two Pressurized Water Reactors (KKNPP 1 and 2) use enriched uranium as fuel. They generate electricity by fission of U-235 and also convert U-238 to plutonium-239.

In the second stage, Fast Breeder Reactors (FBRs) use a mixed fuel made from plutonium-239 (recovered by reprocessing of spent fuel from the first stage) and uranium 238. In FBRs, Plutonium-239 undergoes fission to produce energy, while the uranium-238 present in the mixed fuel transmutes to additional plutonium-239. Thus, the stage-II FBRs are designed to 'breed' more fuel than they consume. India had developed a fast breeder test reactor (FBTR) at Kalpakkam in Tamil Nadu in 1985 and has been operating it since then. A prototype fast breeder reactor (PFBR) of capacity 500 MW has been constructed at Kalpakkam and is expected to be commissioned shortly. Many more such reactors are planned for the near future.

The plan for the third stage is to set up nuclear reactors employing thorium-based (thorium + U-233) fuel. U-233 is produced from thorium in the stage-II FBRs where thorium blanketing of the fuel is done and also in stage-III reactors where thorium is the fertile material. Extensive research and technology development for the third stage is going on and it is expected to be employed for commercial electricity generation only in the later half of this century.

CHAPTER 8

Academics, Research, Technology: The 'Art' in the Knowledge Era

While working as Director, BARC, from 1996 to 2000, and later as Chairman, AEC, I was always struck by the deep thought with which Dr Bhabha had created the ecosystem for scientific research and technology development; and the way it was heading forward (rather, backward!). I realized that executing the first stage of the programme involving thermal reactors and even the second stage involving fast reactors were great achievements, given the fact that the entire technology was developed by us indigenously, in a self-reliant way, in spite of severe technology restrictions by foreign countries. In some cases we even did some new innovative technological development all by ourselves. Yet the fact remained that by and large we were replicating models developed by others.

I sensed that the third stage, which is based on thorium, would be more challenging in terms of addressing the issues involved and developing the most optimal technologies. There is no proven and credible model that can serve as an example in this case. Clearly, the third stage would require more originality, both in the development of concepts as well as in decision-making. This would also need rapid translation from de-novo development to robust commercial application. While I had launched a comprehensive development programme for thorium, our readiness—or lack of it—in doing such things at the required scale and speed always bothered me. Why was it that we, by and large, tend to look for things to emulate? On an impulse, I reversed the question. What were the new core technologies that had been developed in recent times in India for the first time ever, ahead of any other country? Sadly, I could not find a satisfactory answer to that.

Lt. Gen. (Dr) V.J. Sundaram, who had led the Prithvi missile development and deployment programme, used to visit us frequently at BARC. At that time, he was busy building robustness of technology in our strategic programmes. He brought to my notice that research on quantum wells had reached a point where one could soon expect, in the market, highly sensitive quantum well infrared photo-detectors[15]with high application value. He also mentioned that Tata Institute of Fundamental Research (TIFR) was at the forefront of this research, and groups should be set up between TIFR and BARC scientists to take up the development of such photo-detectors in the country. General Sundaram saw an opportunity for development of an important technology with strategic applications that would be on par with other developments taking place in the world at large. We decided to begin work on that. But to my dismay, I found it almost impossible. If you had a scientist who understood the theory, he couldn't engineer the product. And if you had an engineer who

[15]A new technique for thermal imaging that is far more sensitive and has applications in night vision as well as several other areas.

could design the product, he wouldn't understand the science behind it. Making the two groups work together had its own challenges in the absence of the correct individual mindsets and institutional values.

Similarly, the accelerators and fusion reactors needed several high-power microwave systems. This subject used to be taught in our colleges a few decades ago. Slowly this ebbed, being reduced to the low-power microwaves used in telecommunications. Gradually, this too lost its appeal for young students. But the problem remained—how could India move forward in technologies like accelerators and fusion systems? You would need high-power microwave engineering specialists in large numbers to make progress in such frontier areas of technology.

We were already a participant in the development of the International Thermonuclear Experimental Reactor (ITER) project. Equipment worth a few thousand crore was being manufactured for the ITER project in the country. The aim had been to internalize the full domain of technologies involved in fusion energy through our participation in ITER project. Now where do you find experts in adequate numbers who can realize this? It is not part of the curriculum for engineering students. The science postgraduates who might understand the science behind the technology will normally hesitate to work on the large-scale engineering projects, unless they are specifically trained. How do you solve this conundrum?

I struggled hard to find a solution. Once, Prof. P. Rama Rao, who was then Chairman of the AERB, and I were returning from Vienna. We had a four-hour transit halt at Frankfurt. I utilized the time in brainstorming on the ways to strengthen synergy between science and technology for the common goals of the Department. We realized that the problem was related to our education system as well as the value system in our institutions—

both in terms of what and how we teach, and the culture we inculcate. Isolation between teaching and research, and research and its translation to robust technology products—silos created by hierarchical mindsets—appeared to be the core problems. We need a culture where we are able to translate frontline research in science to state-of-the-art technology. This thought was the seed for the creation of the Homi Bhabha National Institute (HBNI) and the kind of structure that we should be adopting at our research institutions.

However, even before the idea of HBNI had taken root, it was decided, after a lot of discussion, to set up a deemed University in TIFR—which came into existence in 2002. This ensured that the link between research and teaching got restored to some extent. However, the larger issues of linking research with both teaching and technology development still remained unsolved.

RESTORING BHABHA'S LEGACY

The Old Yacht Club (OYC) building, next to the Gateway of India in Mumbai, has a special place in the history of Atomic Energy. I had attended a number of meetings and events in the building and heard several more stories of historical importance from some of the old timers. I had attended one of my promotion interviews there, when Ramanna was Director, BARC, and Sethna the Chairman, AEC. Sethna was also the Chairman of the selection committee. The relation between the two was strained. I, however, had done enough work to have made good impressions on both of them. Nevertheless, Ramanna appeared apprehensive about my fate, perhaps because of their mutual relations. He actually called me out from the waiting room to his room a couple of times, essentially to cheer me up. I could understand his concern for me but was amused all the same. In the interview, Sethna said that he knew my work and there was no need for a prolonged discussion. My interview was a cakewalk.

Sometime in the '70s, the staff at the OYC building had noticed that the floor was sinking. This led to a scare that the old building was unsafe. Immediately, the building was evacuated into an adjoining, newly constructed matchbox architecture that was a complete contrast to OYC. Subsequently, there were several discussions about demolishing the old building. Apparently, heritage activists came in the way and saved the building. The building remained unused for a long time and consequently began decaying.

Sudha Bhave, the then joint secretary in the Department, put forth the idea of restoration of the heritage building. We decided to restore the building to its past glory. A heritage architect was engaged and a project for renovation was launched. During inspection, the mystery of the shaking floor was finally unravelled. The shaking floor had originally been built as a dance floor, with springs underneath. Over the years, tons of filing cabinets being piled up on the floor made it lose its vibrancy. As the heavy bureaucratic load of the filing cabinets was removed, the springs expanded and the floor regained its normalcy. The building was not only restored to exactly what it had been, but the portion that had been earlier dismantled was also reconstructed. OYC had regained its past glory.

I made plans to use the renovated building in a manner consistent with the ambience it provided. An effective think tank, policy development activities, broad-based consultation meetings, public engagement and archives were identified as key functions to be carried out from the heritage building, to ensure that it did not fall into disuse again. It was also decided that no bureaucratic offices would be set up there. The Strategic Planning Group

(SPG) was created around that time to prepare us to deal with the major international engagements that were to follow. SPG was envisaged to be able to also deal with other, emerging aspects of social, commercial and human resources-related activities. I asked S.K. Malhotra, the then head of Public Awareness Division (PAD), to take charge of the building and furnish it accordingly. A permanent exhibition on the ground floor of the building with separate entry for the general public, especially school children, was also planned. The lawn facing the seafront could have an area for the visiting children to play and have their lunch. On the other side of the building, I intended to create archives—a long-felt need in DAE. The only staff allowed to move to this building were PAD, SPG and the Chairman's office.

I was passionate about creating and maintaining meaningful archives in the new building. In fact, Dr Bhabha was meticulous about documenting his actions, with records written in a very succinct manner. A comprehensive collection of his file noting would be an important piece of the legacy of science management in DAE, if not in the country. I have noticed that although he seemed to have done many things that are seemingly impossible today, a reading of his file noting demonstrates that there was nothing arbitrary about his actions. They were, in fact, fully consistent with the rules. We need to preserve this heritage.

I recollect reading some of his noting related to performance appraisals of BARC scientific personnel and related documentation, in the Annual Confidential Reports. It was a folded, legal-sized integral document that contained a record of the officer concerned and the work done on one side, and the final assessment by higher levels in the chain of command on the other. Interspersed in between were assessments by all the individuals the officer had worked with, in loose assessment sheets. The idea of having loose assessment sheets was to encourage the officer to work with different seniors, who may not be in his or her line of command. The immediate superior, to whom the officer reported, would make the final assessment after consolidating remarks made on all of the loose sheets. It was designed to promote cross-hierarchical interaction and cooperative work. Over the years this concept was lost. As Director, BARC, I felt strongly about this loss and issued a notice sighting Dr Bhabha and stressing on a revival of the old culture. Sadly, it did not find many takers. I understand that a new format has now been implemented, which is more in tune with bureaucratic administration but lacks the spirit of science management, group research, etc.

Like any prestigious institution, DAE needs to maintain the legacy and culture nurtured by its visionary founder. However, we were far from having what could be called a good archive. Even the book *Atomic Energy in India: 50 Years*, which was created on the occasion of fifty years of our atomic energy programme, looked more like a progress report—which many subsequently criticized. We were able to carry on, essentially driven by the passion of a few individuals that the records of historical importance could be accessed. Most of the old files were kept in gunny bags dumped in a godown in Anushaktinagar. Though we did try to retrieve key documents to be brought into the archives, we did not succeed as the effort could not be kept up for too long.

TIFR and Tata Memorial Centre (TMC) have been very good at maintaining institutional records. The books on their history have been crafted by professionals and are outstanding. The archives at TIFR are wonderful. To understand archives, I even visited Tata Central Archives at Pune. I spent an entire day going around and studying the archives. This was the reason I entrusted TIFR with the task of setting up archives at the OYC building after it had been renovated.

I still believe that DAE, which has been the site of action for much of the atomic energy development in the country, must do more to preserve its history—and that one day, good archives will be established in OYC. With the restoration of the OYC building, the edifice of atomic energy heritage in India may have been restored, but the soul, it seems, is yet to be rediscovered.

Both TIFR and BARC were conceived by Dr Bhabha. Though the two organizations were created by him around the same time, they differed significantly in their organizational structures. TIFR's structure was rather flat, more like an academic institution, whereas BARC's structure was hierarchical, on the lines of a typical national laboratory. Programmes in both institutions were being executed with a holistic approach and with several collaborative links between them, with equal emphasis on basic research and technology. However, over a period of time, both institutions drifted away from what they had been in the beginning. Initially, TIFR was also engaged in the development of new technology. Several technological firsts in the country were created at TIFR, including computers, radars, etc. With time, the values changed—at least for a significant part of the community—and emphasis on technology was diluted.

At BARC, the reverse happened. BARC primarily became an institution engaged in large technology projects. Even teaching and engagement with educational institutions, which earlier used to be done hand in hand with research, slowly got diluted in the name of the perceived distraction it was allegedly causing in the mainstream activity. Some course-correction was done by leveraging the Board of Research in Nuclear Sciences (BRNS) to link research within DAE and that in external institutions/universities through collaboration.

In BARC, science and technology do go hand in hand, being physically located at the same place. However, being primarily a technology institution with a hierarchical structure, scientists wishing to pursue open-ended research addressing important questions tend to become second-class citizens, just like experts pursuing technology at TIFR. Dr Bhabha had set up a system at BARC wherein a scientist could work in multiple groups, quite diverse from each other, and his or her work would be evaluated by peers and subsequently recognized. This system has been diluted over time. The hierarchical grip over the institution has not allowed it to flourish. Hopefully, HBNI would help correct the situation.

There was yet another reason behind setting up the HBNI. Soon after taking over the leadership role in atomic energy, in a meeting with Prime Minister Atal Bihari Vajpayee, I raised the issue of the need for a new BARC-like research centre at a geographically diverse location. I explained to him that presently the strategic facilities were centred in Mumbai, and a single strike by the enemy would annihilate the nuclear capability of the country for decades. It was not wise to put all eggs in one basket. Since BARC is located on the west coast, another should be planned on the east coast. He promptly agreed and said, 'Find a place'. That was the beginning of the new campus for BARC near Vizag. The Andhra Pradesh Government was very cooperative; the new campus that is taking shape there will be much bigger than BARC. Here was a chance to make a course-correction in our thinking in terms of organizing science institutions based on past experience.

HBNI, which encompassed all other DAE institutions engaged in research and was an attempt to promote the research-technology linkage, came into being mid-2005. At HBNI, we would encourage students to work on the interface of cutting-edge science and technology, with an aim to prepare a new breed of experts who could work to develop new technologies out of new science. Over a period of time, one could expect such a qualified pool to grow.

Activities like the development, construction and operation of reactors, plants for nuclear fuel cycle and, other key materials, large-scale radiation technology applications, etc. would involve coordinated and time-bound efforts. They would need to be structured in the new campus the way it is happening now in BARC at Trombay. However, the programmes in disciplines like physics, chemistry, biology, materials science, different engineering disciplines, etc. have to be pursued with a focus on expanding the frontiers of these disciplines and widening their scope to include interdisciplinary opportunities, while they contribute to the technology programme. They must thus be organized in an academic framework. It has thus emerged that these programmes at Vizag should be pursued primarily within the HBNI umbrella, even though the infrastructural support is provided by the central administration of the centre. While the national lab and the academic frameworks would be connected at the top, in terms of major programme thrusts, resource allocation etc., they could pursue their different frameworks autonomously, with individual scientists choosing which side he or she would like to be on. While they would be judged accordingly, there would be freedom to work on the other side as well.

Hopefully, this dream will see the light of day sooner rather than later, and Bhabha's legacy of pursuing research and technology development together with a high level of synergy and excellence will be restored.

I remember discussing the need for stronger research in the back-end of the nuclear fuel cycle and the role HBNI could play, over and above the work that was already in progress at BARC and IGCAR. Baldev Raj, the then director of IGCAR, played an important role. A committee under his leadership was entrusted with the task of identifying areas where there were gaps in our capability, in the back-end of the nuclear fuel cycle. It focused on gaps where the Department would need development of additional technologies, particularly in the second and third stage of India's nuclear power programme. Based on the study by the committee, a large basket of topics for PhD was created. The doctoral students at HBNI would have a choice of research topics from the basket. That way, both the students and the Department stood to gain.

Prof. J.B. Joshi joining HBNI after he completed his tenure as Director of Institute of Chemical Technology (ICT) in 2009 was a big boost for both HBNI and DAE. Earlier, we had started a large collaborative programme with ICT that encompassed various aspects of improving chemical engineering processes in DAE plants through detailed simulations. Under the programme, a large number of students could pursue PhD level research on topics related to these subjects. This mechanism worked well. Prof. J.B. Joshi had made, and continues to make, valuable contributions towards this endeavour. One day, I was taking a stroll at Matheran, a popular hill station not far from Mumbai. I stumbled upon Prof. Joshi, along with Mrs Joshi and a bunch of students in tow. I asked what he was doing in a holiday resort along with his students. He replied that he was on an excursion. He and his entourage were walking, observing the beauty of nature and discussing the research undertaken by the students. He is a modern epitome of the 'gurukul', the ancient Indian way of teaching and learning.

HBNI came into existence to fulfil the needs of the R&D centres of DAE as well as to improve the research culture at the new campus of BARC. Simultaneously, it was necessary to pay attention to improving the quality of higher education in science to produce good researchers. Thus an initiative for a five-year integrated course in science education, leading to an MSc degree, was also started. The intention was to promote high-quality science education in an environment of high-quality research. Alongside the several Indian Institutes of Science Education and Research (IISERs) that came up in the country, DAE was tasked to set up a parallel National Institute of Science Education and Research (NISER) at Bhubaneswar. Yet another parallel effort was made to do something similar in an existing, old university, leveraging the strengths of the faculty and institutions in proximity. This was done in the form of the DAE-Mumbai University Centre of Excellence in Basic Sciences (DAE-MU CEBS) at the Kalina campus of the university. This model has the added advantage of positively influencing academics in an existing university at much lower costs. Bringing professionals together, though a big plus, is also a big challenge that has been successfully managed at Kalina. The setting up of NISER as well as DAE-MU CEBS was a joy and a great learning experience.

While the organizational framework is important in promoting a conducive environment for scientists to work in, it is the expectation of values as reflected in individual assessments that drive the individuals in their pursuits. Congruence between the organization goals and these values embedded in individual appraisals is, to my mind, the key to successfully realizing all-round excellence. The yardstick for measurement of excellence should thus reflect a rightly weighted combination of performance in different domains such as research, technology and teaching, with research contributing to new knowledge, technology contributing to value, and teaching contributing to development of human resources. While all three must coexist, their relative weightage should depend on organizational objectives. The translation, however, must be guaranteed wherever there is an opportunity, either by the parent institution itself or together with other collaborative institutions.

Dr Bhabha had set up and nurtured BARC Training School as a key human resource endeavour. I believe that the human resource challenge in today's world of rapidly changing technology is even more demanding. The measures listed above will hopefully be useful in addressing this challenge. Nobody is going to join hands with us as an equal collaborator in any area of technology unless we have some unique core strength in the field. If we do not have that minimum strength in the area, we are more likely to be exploited. Research, technology, education and human capacity-building should thus go hand in hand. I remember that once I had asked Dr Ramanna for guidance in the context of a collaboration proposal that had come to me from a foreign group. Having experienced the restrictive attitude of foreign entities, I had developed a sceptical mindset about such proposals. 'How strong are we in the area?,' Dr Ramanna asked. 'Reasonably strong,' I replied. His final advice was profound. 'You should be careful and be protective of your group in the early phase of development, as that is where harm can come. That attitude should, however, change once a minimum strength is built up. Engaging with external groups at that stage will make you stronger.'

CHAPTER 9

Creating Wealth in Rural India

Grameen Vikas or development of rural India is something that excites me, and I experience a great joy in sharing my ideas in this field. Dr Sharad Pawar and Dr Rannaware of BARC were experts in plant breeding and biopesticides respectively. They were coordinating the BARC seed development programme along with agricultural universities. Crop varieties were regularly being developed in BARC in collaboration with these universities, and were getting notified after the multilocational field trials. This had been one of the successful programmes of BARC, with significant societal impact. The demand for breeder seeds of these varieties was continuously growing. When I was Director, BARC, they approached me for help in meeting the increased requirement of breeder seeds. Together, we visited almost all agricultural universities in Maharashtra, and some outside, to seek collaboration for increased production of breeder seeds. Whenever we requested university experts for it though, they would invariably ask for corresponding enhancement of the grant from BARC. We agreed to provide the required money, but a question lingered in my mind. The breeder seeds were meant to contribute to seed production, which leads to higher agricultural production. Thus, if cultivation is expected to yield returns for farmers, seed production should lead to higher returns and breeder seed production should give even higher benefits. Breeder seed production should therefore be an income proposition. Why was it that more money was required to produce larger quantities? Should that not be the other way round?

When I enquired with a vice chancellor of an agricultural university, he explained the dynamics of breeder seeds in India. Seeds could only be sold at a controlled price—and that too, to a corporation of the state government. The university did not receive adequate money to compensate for the cost incurred. I raised this issue with the Ministry of Agriculture in the central government. They were aware of the issue. We were advised that we need not restrict ourselves to agricultural universities. We were encouraged to work with private entities. We were directed to approach the small farmers' consortium. We were also told to teach farming, including quality control, to progressive farmers and encourage them to take up breeder seed cultivation. As a result, the breeder seed production quickly went up manyfold. In fact, a progressive farmer, Jayakumar Gunde, set a national record (and a world record of sorts) in groundnut production. It was a matter of great satisfaction that research at BARC was making significant impact in rural India. We were motivated to do more.

THE AKRUTI-CILLAGE ECOSYSTEM

To embark on an organized engagement with the rural domain, my colleague A.M. Patankar developed a concept—the Advanced Knowledge-based Rural Technology Initiative (AKRUTI). It is an initiative wherein scientists from BARC work in cooperation with non-government organizations (NGOs) to familiarize villagers with a range of technologies developed in BARC that can make a difference to their livelihoods. An AKRUTI tech-pack was configured for this purpose. I liked the concept. I also felt that the idea should be implemented in a manner that would assure sustenance of the activity once it was started. We could not be starting an activity that permanently depended on doles or grants. I suggested to Patankar that we should approach an external funding agency rather than using DAE funds, and test out the realization of sustainability over a given period of time. Approaching external funding agencies also had the advantage of an independent scrutiny. If the agencies found merit in AKRUTI, then we could ask them for one funding cycle, at the end of which it should become self-supporting. The model had to support itself if it was to succeed in the long run.

We approached Vasant Gowarikar, who was chairing the Rajiv Gandhi Science & Technology Commission (RGSTC) at that time. The Commission approved funding of three AKRUTIs at Chiplun, Pali and Amravati in the state of Maharashtra. During review of these projects, it emerged that although they had not attained complete self-sustainability, there were indications that in the long run they could stand on their own feet. This initiative gave us the confidence that sustainable models for deployment of technologies in a rural setting, to enhance the livelihood of people, would be feasible.

The AKRUTI model exposed rural people to new technologies. However, if the technology remained static, then it would become obsolete and non-competitive with time. Technologies need to be kept updated to a state-of-the-art level. This needs R&D within the rural domain. Engineering colleges or universities that are in the neighbourhood can help in serving this purpose. Such knowledge centres can also train individuals to solve technological problems, or even create new technologies. That way, while the knowledge institution sees a significant upgrade, the technology will constantly be rejuvenated and livelihoods will be sustainable. The youth can also explore avenues for development that can benefit the rural economy. They can even get into entrepreneurship. Some of the additional opportunities in rural areas are:

a) Farm services and value addition to agro-produce to manufacture food and non-food products.
b) Decentralized watershed management, manufacture of devices for potable water, clean-up of waste water and effluents.
c) Smokeless kitchens that are environmentally sustainable.
d) Decentralized energy production (biomass, solar, wind, etc.) and utilization (solar lights, microgrids, solar drying).
e) Manufacture of small agri-implements for use on small and marginal farms, including for irrigation and crop protection.
f) Knowledge products that cater to local as well as global needs.
g) Other value addition activities based on local as well as imported raw material that leverage local human resources.

We also started pondering on the ways to expand this experience to address the larger issue of bridging urban-rural disparity. Nearly two-thirds of the Indian population lives in villages. Although agriculture is the mainstay of rural economy, only one-third of rural households are able to live on farm income. The remaining households are either landless, or their landholdings are too small to support their livelihoods. Roughly half of the rural households persist on manual casual labour. Average rural income is about half of the average urban income. Soil quality in the farmlands is constantly degrading, and the agricultural yield has remained low. Allied activities like dairy, animal husbandry, poultry, other cottage industries, etc. supplement the livelihoods of the rural populace.

On the other hand, while there are greater opportunities for livelihoods in cities, urban India is characterized by highly stressed infrastructure. The growth of slums, transportation woes, crises in solid-waste management and stormwater drainage, and rising pollution are some indicators of this, to name but a few. Even so, it is the difference in opportunities that drives people to migrate from villages to cities. This phenomenon perhaps occurs the fastest in India among the larger countries. We are currently embracing the knowledge era, where knowledge technologies promote democratization and decentralization. Thus, the knowledge era offers equal opportunities in urban and rural domains. While agriculture and related activities remain in the rural domain, the manufacturing sector is no longer the prerogative of the urban habitat. Similarly, the logistics and service sector is fast moving to the rural domain. The rural youth can be adequately trained to leverage these opportunities with appropriate facilitation, through which the disparity between the urban and rural domains can be significantly reduced and consequently migration can be slowed down, if not totally arrested. In fact, in future, one can expect higher opportunities in the rural domain as compared to the urban domain. The added attractions of rural life are a higher level of happiness, respectability, and a clean and green environment. How does one achieve this goal? The key is knowledge empowerment of the rural population, especially the youth.

A notable feature of migration dynamics is movement of organic matter from farms to cities and inorganic matter from factories to farms in increasing quantities. This is causing problems of depletion of organic carbon in farm soils and increased bacterial pollution in air and water in urban areas. This leads to low water retention, poor nutrient uptake and lower productivity in agricultural lands, and problems of solid-waste management, higher transportation costs and a heavy burden of public health management in urban areas. Reversing or arresting migration by raising rural income and reclaiming organic carbon in the form of manure obtained by processing biodegradable municipal solid waste in urban areas is thus a strategy that would benefit both rural and urban areas. The key, as mentioned above, is to look at models for rural areas, which go well beyond agriculture. They should be capable of providing earnings comparable to urban areas over a broader spectrum of activities, including those in manufacturing and service segments.

In this context, we came up with the concept of Cillage (city + village). This went far beyond Providing Urban Amenities to Rural Areas (PURA), which Dr Abdul Kalam had proposed. PURA aimed at providing urban amenities like drinking water, street lights, education, healthcare and telecom services in the rural areas. Cillage is based on three elements—knowledge, technology and livelihood. These elements engage, interact and synergize with each other. There had been such initiatives in the past, but they focused on any one of these elements at a time—not all three together.

Cillage aims to be a knowledge bridge between city and village, which can reduce the knowledge gradient and enthuse and empower people to create value by addressing local problems and exploiting opportunities. The aim would be to create a knowledge-based ecosystem for integrated education, research, and technology development and deployment, as well as capacity building in rural areas.

A model of Cillage was demonstrated with the help of a public-private partnership project. Several organizations came together, with each playing a complementary role. Shri Vithal

Education and Research Institute (SVERI) at Gopalpur (near Pandharpur in Maharashtra) offered to host the project. RGSTC decided to fund the project. A Rural Human and Resource Development Facility (RHRDF) was set up at SVERI, wherein an AKRUTI tech-pack provided by BARC was deployed. BARC scientists trained staff and villagers at RHRDF as well as at a number of AKRUTI centres that were set up in villages around SVERI. This helped in the understanding and use of technologies. At RHRDF, the activities went beyond familiarization and training, and slowly encompassed manufacturing and production. SVERI started looking into making improvements to the existing technologies—and even creating new ones.

Today, SVERI has become the go-to place for rural engineering colleges in search of projects. They hold regular expos on various projects relevant to the rural domain. In the process, R&D at SVERI has itself become innovative. SVERI has also conducted a few international conferences on 'Techno-Social', a theme aimed at transforming the rural domain through technologies. Knowledge, technology and livelihood demonstration are at work together at the Gopalpur Cillage.

A NEW DIGITAL PARADIGM

But what about the younger generation? While engaging elderly people would help enhance their livelihoods, the opportunities provided by the knowledge era are much wider. Enagaging rural students while they are still in school, to prepare them for the knowledge era, would be most effective. With this objective in mind, it was planned to add a school education segment in Gopalpur Cillage. A National Knowledge Network (NKN) node was established at SVERI by P.S. Dekhne of BARC. Prof. M.V. Pitke, formerly of TIFR, with assistance from a private firm, set up a low-cost, long-range broadband wireless transmitter at SVERI. This enabled schools within a 20-km radius to access education resources and other relevant material through digital connectivity. Five schools were connected. The MKCL Knowledge Foundation is a section 8 company of Maharashtra Knowledge Corporation Limited, an Information Technology (IT) firm with an agenda for social transformation. Along with Indian Consortium for Educational Transformation (I-CONSENT) and Homi Bhabha Centre for Science Education (HBCSE), they developed Open Education Resources (OERs) in the Marathi language for secondary schools.[16] This endeavour enabled a new technology-powered holistic school education framework alongside delivery of a prescribed school curriculum in a non-intrusive manner. Attempts have been made to turn this into a support feature that complements the efforts of teachers, and thereby transform the system of education in rural schools through an internal pull. I do believe that MKCL can take this to its logical end and make a huge difference to the school education scene in the country. Under a separate programme, a two-year PG Diploma in E-education in Digital Society (PG-DEEDS) has been developed for teachers' education, consistent with the new digital paradigm set by MKCLKF, Yashwantrao Chavan Maharashtra Open University (YCMOU) and I-CONSENT. Deep thinking and implementation efforts by Prof. Ram Takwale and Vivek Sawant lie behind these initiatives.

By now we know that a Cillage-AKRUTI ecosystem with a built-in school education component can be implemented in a self-sustaining mode. While Gopalpur Cillage at SVERI was progressing on its own steam, another initiative was started in Gadchiroli district of Maharashtra, which is predominantly a tribal

[16]These are now accessible to everyone at http://mahadnyan.mkcl.org/.

area. I advised the Gondwana University, Gadchiroli (GUG), the new upcoming University in the area, that this was an opportunity to do something new. GUG planned to establish a Science and Technology Resource Centre (STRC) as a centre of excellence. The centre was to have complete autonomy and would focus on a) mapping of the resources of the region, especially forests, b) exploring the kind of livelihood opportunities that could be created, c) providing for capacity building for the local people of the region and d) developing academic programmes in the university that would address the local requirements. GUG and STRC are both currently under development. The project is picking up steam and the results will be seen in the future.

RHRDF-SVERI and STRC-GUG are experiments that demonstrate the concept of Cillage under two distinctly different scenarios. It is necessary to scale this experiment to the block level. That is the smallest unit that can be linked with the government machinery for credible action. Local endeavours to steer economic activity, duly empowered by knowledge, should enable local capacity that is adequate enough to plan development and influence government schemes for area development. This will help in creating a happy and competent society that does not have to look to cities. We have thus started discussing an experiment at the block level in Nandurbar, again a tribal area in Maharashtra.

These initiatives are moving at their own pace; I am not pushing them hard. I want the idea to take root and sink into the minds of people. There has to be a buy-in from within—only then can such projects be sustainable. My aim is to create models that can be replicated.

CHAPTER 10

Knowledge-empowered Ecosystems

Institutions are among the four important pillars of an enlightened and competitive society, the other pillars being infrastructure, technology and a system of motivation or incentives. Governance of institutions thus deserves much greater attention than it usually gets. Important among institutions are those that deal with human resource-development, knowledge-generation and dissemination, technology and empowerment of the weaker sections of the society.

The way we deal with our institutions, particularly the public-funded ones, is something that has been bothering me for a long time. If we look at the rankings of global universities, we will find that most of the educational institutions at the top of the table have maintained their high level of excellence over very long periods of time. Universities like Cambridge and Oxford are between eight hundred to a thousand years old. In India, too, we had the renowned Nalanda University, which was established in the fifth century BCE and thrived till about 1200 CE, when it was burnt down. Thus, if organized well, there is evidence that institutions can maintain high levels of excellence over very long periods of time. In contrast, barring a few exceptions, our present-day institutions tend to decay after they reach a steady state. We need to understand why this happens. While creating a new institution, it is important to ensure that principles of good governance are imbibed by both the institution and its stakeholders. In the formative years of an institution, resources are available, the institution is in its growth phase, and there is ample enthusiasm. The acid test for a good governance framework is to sustain relevance and excellence when the institution is in a steady state over long period. Every institution should have a clearly defined mission in terms of what they deliver to society. The value system of the institution should be developed and imbibed in a manner that is consistent with its mission.

Generally, institutions are of two kinds. One is where you deliver a service based on a set of rules and procedures. In such cases, the activities involved are fairly routine. The other kind are those that are engaged in creative pursuits. While they do need a framework for functioning, their activities are far from routine, and need new approaches all the time. We need to understand that while a conformal setup is necessary for organized working, creativity is the key to human progress. The two must coexist healthily without causing damage to each other. The two types of organizations thus cannot be governed identically. In the government, you have departments meant for administration, maintenance of law and order, etc. on one side; and departments meant for national development, including those involved in science and research, on the other. I often feel that a common set of rules of governance or a common framework for dealing with all of them, as is the case at present, causes more harm than good.

This differentiation is even more important in the context of dealing with personnel. While appraisal and recognition frameworks in routine activities could be based on quantitative measures and managed within the hierarchy, such modes of appraisal would certainly kill creativity and promote mediocrity in organizations engaged in creative pursuits. Judgement by peers in the domain of individual assessment should be of paramount importance. There is evidence that setting quantitative targets to incentivize creative performance damages creativity itself and should be avoided. Unfortunately, things seem to be moving in this direction.

The governance framework of the institution should be determined, formulated and put in practice by a peer community with high credibility. The peers should share the same kind of mission and values, and should be identified on the basis of their past performance and track records. They should be both from within the system and outside, representing all stakeholders. Autonomy in governance is of paramount importance and is the key to excellence in all creative endeavours. Thus there must be sufficient flexibility for decision making and action at all levels within the prescribed limits. Discussion, analysis and decision making should be a comprehensive process involving the building of consensus among all stakeholders, and should be done with an open mind.

The aforementioned autonomy should be incorporated in the institution's constitution. This should be respected and upheld by all stakeholders. Autonomy means that the system is able to manage by itself, but it does not mean that there is no accountability. The degree of accountability at different levels should also be specified and monitored by the peers. Regardless of which entities provide resources, the peers should have a key say in the affairs of the institution. Owners of the institution, after having specified top-level goals and objectives, also need to respect the autonomy of their institutions if they seek to nurture creative pursuits. They could invoke emergency powers if, in very rare situations, this becomes unavoidable.

Availability of sufficient finance and other resources are also important factors in facilitating a high level of excellence. While the ability of the institution to raise resources outside the funds provided by the owner/promoter is an important factor in protecting autonomy, the onus of ensuring the supply of the originally promised funds should be on the owner/promoter. Though the ability to raise resources is an indicator of the competitive performance of the institution, unmindful insistence on raising external resources when the opportunity for the same does not exist could drive the institution away from the originally intended objectives. The institutions should be free to develop their programmes so long as they are consistent with the institutional mandate and within the available financial resources, as long as there is no new additional recurring expenditure in future. This could go beyond what has been already approved or what can be managed with the resources raised by the institution. While incurring the expenditure out of public funds (government funding), one has to follow the broad canons of financial propriety as provided for in the government rules. However, the tendency to micromanage institutions through mindless application of government rules should be both curbed and resisted.

Dilution of autonomy and consequent degradation of excellence usually begins through such tendencies to straitjacket institutions. We have well accepted diversity as a key principle in the sustainability and nurturing of nature. I believe that the same holds true for the knowledge and creativity domain.

The head of the institution has a major role in this respect. He has to be the custodian and protector of the autonomy. He is also accountable to the stakeholders—those who provide resources and benefit from the institution. At times, the head of the organization may have conflicting interests to balance. He has to protect the autonomy and governance based on peer processes on one hand, and address the justifiable expectations of the stakeholders on the other. The institutional systems need to be built in a manner that prevents conflict between the two. In a way, this is the true test of the leadership.

BEYOND THE POLITICS OF COMPETITIVE APPEASEMENT

At the apex national or state level, we have a good constitution that forms the basis of governance in our country. However, there are issues related to the way governance is implemented. The political part of the executive seems to be excessively involved in the execution of activities, rather than focusing on the formulation of policies and programmes. It is important that there be a separation between the formulation of policies and programmes—on which the political class should focus, and the execution of the programme—which should be left to the professional class. In this, there should be least interference from the political class, or for that matter from bureaucrats. There is also a need to separate the programme formulation activity to be done centrally from that to be done in a decentralized manner. For all local development plans, while broad contours in terms of objectives and overall resource allocation could be done centrally, the details of planning and implementation should be done in a decentralized fashion with local wisdom and expertise playing an important role.

There should be a major capacity-building effort for this purpose, particularly in the local knowledge institutions. These institutions must have a much deeper engagement with local, professional expertise and formulation of local development needs, which should be implemented in the bottom-up mode. The concept of Cillage extending up to the block level could, in my view, be an important factor in the credible and effective formulation and implementation of development plans in the bottom-up mode. Ultimately, all these ideas are embedded in the concept of decentralized development through local self-government. Wherever this has taken place, spectacular results have been seen. The achievement of Popatrao Pawar at Hiware Bazar is a good case in point. The challenge is to make this happen with good governance across the board. Moreover, a knowledge- and technology-empowered society at the grass roots would leave no room for the politics of competitive appeasement using untenable doles, which is causing more harm than good.

I believe that the value systems in our families and society are of paramount importance. The values that are dear to us help us steer ourselves on the right path. A knowledge-empowered society, with the right values, forms its own notions about the right path to follow and develops enough strength to drive things on that path. Going forward, such societies keep us on the right track in the present-day world, which is expected to change at an accelerated pace. Governments, with their inherent inertia, seem increasingly incapable of dealing with rapidly developing oncoming problems. That act is more likely to be an impulsive one in the reactive mode. Therefore, we need to nurture an ecosystem in our societies that is knowledge-empowered, in a holistic way. That is the reason why I devote a lot of time these days to Cillage development and to education.

CHAPTER 11

Beyond the Classroom: Holistic Education

Education is a vast domain and is about development of effective and capable human resources. Several dimensions are involved in this process. While being conscious about one's limitations, it is important that we evolve situation-specific solutions rather than attempting a single straitjacketed solution.

I realized the importance of education while in DAE and was equally concerned about our ability to create new technologies by quickly translating new findings in scientific research. The setting up of HBNI, NISER and DAE-MU-CEBS was the result. Working with IIT Bombay for around a decade-and-a-half made me aware of several aspects of high-quality technical education. However, over a period of time, I realized that the problem of education in the country is much deeper and needs attention across the entire domain: early childhood care and education, primary education, secondary education as well as higher education and research. It has to do with the development of an attitude towards dealing with knowledge—both to expand its frontiers and to leverage it for creating value. I have come to the conclusion that this is more of a cultural problem that we have ignored for too long. Let me explain.

If we study the lists of top import and export items in India, we will find that both lists are almost identical, with a balance of payments that is not in our favour. Take for example, iron and steel. Despite being rich in raw materials and having a large steel industry in the country, we seem to be importing much more than what we are able to export. For a country that has the heritage of the 'Rustless Wonder', the iron pillar of Delhi, this should trigger deep soul-searching. This deficiency in terms of competitive value addition in the country in most areas is a cause for concern. I strongly believe that this is the result of a disconnect between the country's scientific research and technology development efforts. There are, however, notable exceptions. For example, vehicles, pharmaceuticals and clothing are areas where our exports exceed our imports. There are good examples of significant industry investment in R&D in these areas. So, in principle, things *can* happen in our country.

The problem, in my view, is the silo mentality that binds us. There seems to be an underlying belief that academics and industry cannot mix—that doing so degrades excellence. Academics is considered to be above industrial activity. Industry, on the other hand, doubts—perhaps justifiably—the capability of academia in solving their problems. This mentality prevents us from growing as an innovative society. Now that we are in the knowledge era, we can ill afford this situation. We need to look at education at all levels to remedy this challenge.

We need a cultural transformation where we address this issue on multiple levels. The conventional teaching of science experiments in schools is structured with well-formulated steps and conclusions at the end, much like a production line. This may be necessary, but it is not enough. I have already narrated the efforts to try out a new technology-enabled holistic school education framework. There is a strong element of social engagement and activity-based learning in the framework that is being evolved. Under another initiative at Rajiv Gandhi Science and Technology Commission, Maharashtra (RGSTC), we have launched a scheme for school children. Science and Innovation Activity Centres (SIACs) are modelled on a basis similar to 'Exploratory', conceptualized by Prof. V.G. Bhide. The idea is to create an immersive opportunity for school children in terms of addressing their curiosity and helping them experience the fun of science and the joy of exploration.

This environment of unstructured hands-on activities/ experiments includes debate and mentoring around the principles of science. There exist fairly large national and regional science centres in the country, like the Nehru Science Centre in Mumbai, Birla Science Centre in Hyderabad, Visvesvaraya Science Museum in Bengaluru, Science City in Kolkata, etc. They are mostly in state capitals or large cities. They have large footfalls, but are still inadequate when you look at the number of school children in the country and the level/depth of engagement that is necessary. Under the Atal Innovation Mission (AIM), the Atal Tinkering Labs (ATLs) are being established to encourage innovative thinking among young students. These labs need to grow in number so that more students can experience the excitement of science. However, their scope seems limited.

SIACs effectively bridge the gap between large science centres and small facilities like ATLs, limited to individual schools. SIACs are hosted in large educational institutions and are open to all students in the neighbourhood. They are set up in a public–education institution partnership model, with the onus of sustaining its operation resting with the host institution. School students can spend time in SIACs on multiple occasions and there are opportunities for delivering certain science lessons at the SIACs. National Council for Science Museums (NCSM), along with institutions like HBCSE, Exploratory, and Vidnyanashram, have helped in the operationalization of this scheme. NCSM also has a number of buses equipped with science experiments that can travel between places. In a recent experiment, an NCSM bus visited several villages around Warana, where we have an operating SIAC. The experience shows that an SIAC in every district, and later in every block, along with a lab on wheels, should be able to cover a large section of school children, inculcating a spirit of inquisitiveness and innovation in them.

There is yet another interesting model being followed by Marathi Vidnyan Parishad under the leadership of Prof. J.B. Joshi. The students at the level of junior college (eleventh and twelfth standards) are provided with low-cost kits that can be used to demonstrate school experiments in science disciplines. After an initial orientation, these students visit a particular school (perhaps even their own) on Saturdays and demonstrate the experiments to the younger students. This benefits both the students who teach and those who are being taught. This can be an excellent model of peer-to-peer learning.

SKILLS FOR THE FUTURE

For college students, things have to be done differently. Dr Kalam used to say that every student should pass out from the school with two certificates—one, the basic school-passing certificate; and the other, a 'Skill Certificate'. While in school, there should be an opportunity to learn useful skills in addition to the regular academic curriculum. The same logic could be extended to the college level across all disciplines. One can always uncover skills that are relevant to the academic programme that a student is pursuing. For example, if someone is pursuing a BA in History, then he/she should be able to pick up soft skills that enable working at least as a tourist guide. That would enable the student to earn a livelihood, if necessary, even while studying and also create further interest in history.

Students in engineering colleges face similar issues. Most of these students do projects in industry. These projects are aimed more at getting them familiarized with the industrial scene and less at real-life problem-solving. Micro, Small and Medium Enterprises (MSMEs) constitute an important segment of industry with high employment potential, perhaps dwarfed only by agriculture. They are also large foreign exchange earners. Yet, they suffer from issues of working capital and upgradation of technology. Even when they start with state-of-the-art technology, it becomes obsolete in decades. The world moves at a faster pace than them, and they remain stuck with old technologies and become non-competitive. Their technical problems are mostly well within the capabilities of third- and final-year engineering students. This is thus an excellent opportunity for students to try their hands at real-life problem-solving, and for the industries to get the right human resource to meet their needs.

This win-win situation was leveraged to create an MSME Internship Programme both at Technology Information Forecasting and Assessment Council (TIFAC) and at RGSTC. Under the scheme, students work with industry to identify and plan a problem resolution project that they can address within the time available to them. A few of the best projects thus formulated are selected for actual implementation. Apart from the resources that can be mobilized by the industry and the college, the scheme also provides a grant of up to ₹1 lakh. The students go through a rich learning experience in real life. The programme changes the mindset and improves the problem-solving acumen of the engineering students. In the context of the common refrain about non-employability of engineering students in the country, this is a major gain. A large developing country like India needs engineers with problem-solving capabilities in large numbers. I believe that the MSME internship model is an effective one. It will also develop a better connect between education and industry, and help in making society more innovative.

The absence of the right ecosystem for addressing issues leads to several lost opportunities. The case of the guar bean (cluster bean) is an interesting example. Horizontal drilling and fracking technology have made shale oil and shale gas a reality. The rock is fractured for extraction, which requires a fluid with appropriate viscous properties. It was found that the guar bean could be used to extract guar gum, which in turn could be mixed with water to make an excellent fluid for extraction of shale oil and gas. Americans began importing guar beans and as a result, Indian exports of the bean went up. India became a major supplier of guar beans. Soon enough, middlemen got involved and began short-changing and cutting unfair deals with farmers. Over time, American importers became wary of the difficulties and began sourcing the beans from Brazil and other places, where their cultivation picked up. Consequently, demand for guar beans from India plummeted. Indian farmers began complaining and that is when the government realized the problem and referred it to TIFAC. We at TIFAC carried out a patent search. We found that we were one of the largest producers of guar beans, yet did not hold even 1 per cent of the patents on technologies and processes related to value addition to this raw material. Obviously, our science system had not paid adequate attention to this area. There was a disconnect. Interestingly, on further enquiry it turned out that guar beans with minimum value addition were being exported to China, where significant value addition took place before they were finally exported to the US. China was thus benefitting more than India out of a demand for Indian raw materials in the US.

The production of titanium in India is another telling case. The ilmenite mineral is a vast resource in our beach sands, which is being mined and exported. This mineral is a prime raw material for titanium, a very important metal for our times. Indian Rare Earths Limited (IREL), which is a public sector undertaking under the administrative control of DAE, made several attempts to set up domestic commercial production capacity for value addition on ilmenite, but they did not succeed. We even decided to liberalize the beach sand policy to encourage private sector participation, primarily for setting up value addition plants in the country. Production of the mineral and its export went up, but no commercial value addition plant came up.

On deeper thought it became obvious that the ability to set up commercial titanium production in the country was more of a technology issue. The process is energy-intensive. Energy costs in India are high. Also, the environmental burden linked to such plants located in the coastal zone was unacceptable. I then approached Prof. Joshi, who was then the Director of the Institute of Chemical Technology in Mumbai. I wanted chemical engineers to help in the matter. He, in turn, mentioned this to Dr K.H. Gharda, one of the most innovative entrepreneurs, who has successfully set up a huge industrial empire, Gharda Chemicals, based on his own research. Dr Gharda figured out how to extract titanium, utilizing much less energy and with a lower environmental burden. He developed the process and set up a pilot plant. The project is being pursued for upscaling, through his own investment. There is even a distinct possibility of liquidating the red mud dumps that arise as a result of aluminium production activities and constitute a global environmental issue, along with utilization of ilmenite. Dr Gharda envisaged the possibility of a multi-trillion-dollar industry coming up on the basis of the technology being developed by him. He wanted to explore the possibility of linkages with government entities engaged in aluminium- and titanium-related activities. I have always considered the possibility of such development to be of high national importance. I even wrote a letter to the PMO to explore if this important mission could be pursued in private-public partnership mode. The PMO did send the letter to concerned entities and some discussion did take place. However, it is my belief that the vitiated atmosphere with respect to such joint efforts and the audit-related fears in the minds of people in public institutions did not allow any progress in this regard.

This episode is now several years old. Gharda will soon turn ninety. His efforts continue unabated, but what will happen to India's titanium opportunity, I do not know.

There are many such examples. In my thinking, the problem relates to the mindset of people, an inadequate ecosystem and the distorted values that we are propagating. I believe that the solution lies in improving our education system. We need to nurture an ambience that supports positivity and high values, in which competent youth can confidently move forward and take risks with a professional approach. This is a more serious and difficult challenge than one might imagine. Today, in any discussion with teachers on education, the discourse will invariably tend to be on the problems of teachers rather than the problems of education. We need to develop workable demonstrations that can make a difference in a non-intrusive mode, and promote their broader adoption because of benefits they bring.

CHAPTER 12

The Way Forward

Since Independence in 1947, we have pursued a mixed economy model with a socialist orientation. Although Mahatma Gandhi had stressed on rural empowerment and self-reliance, the agenda for production by the masses could not stand competition from mass production. A creative and healthy mix between the two has been eluding us. The key of economic policies in the nineties did spur the economy, which has been steadily growing at a fast rate since then. However, the issue of disparities, which are perhaps rising, is still a big challenge. A stringent technology embargo was another challenge the country had been facing. After acquiring the indigenous technological capability required for protecting our national security in areas where nobody would ever help us, we are now reasonably integrated with the high-tech world, especially after the opening up of international civil nuclear cooperation. We need to leverage this opportunity to take India to the top of the table in the world. Our demographic dividend—and the world embracing the knowledge era—are of huge importance in this context. The key is to prepare our youth to be among the best performers in the contemporary global arena. We can already see the impact made by our youth wherever this has happened. The challenge is to empower the maximum percentage of our youth to leverage this opportunity.

We must also recognize that knowledge technologies promote both democratization and decentralization. The challenge of reducing disparities can now be better addressed by empowering youth everywhere through the right kind of education, training and human development. The nature of jobs is changing very fast. Several traditional jobs are likely to be taken over by machines. Humans have to be prepared to engage themselves at much higher levels of creative and productive activities. The challenge is to make the right education accessible to the youth of the country, and this challenge has to be addressed on a war footing. Not doing so in time could have disastrous consequences for the country in the present-day competitive world.

We, thus, have a dual challenge. The first challenge is to withstand global competition, and the other is orderly socio-economic transformation—wherein people at the grass roots are empowered to exploit the new opportunity. This is where I consider the Cillage development programmes in rural areas to be relevant and urgent. They will enhance livelihood, provide education to build the capacity of people in the new context, and facilitate research to rejuvenate existing technologies and even build new ones.

India has a large population, which soon might overtake China's. The gap between our per capita energy use and that required to assure a quality of life for her people comparable with advanced countries, is much larger than that of China. Thus, India's additional energy needs are the largest compared to any other country in the world. India's rapidly growing economy would, in fact, create the demand for this growth. We therefore need to secure our long-term energy access at a level commensurate with our aspirations. While doing so, we also need to address the challenge of climate change. Luckily for us, both energy security and climate change point to the inevitability of nuclear and solar energy. Both of these are non-fossil energy sources. Renewable energy—particularly solar energy—is important. However, most renewable energy sources are variable. Grid stability cannot be assured in a viable manner without base load generation being a significant component.[17]

Nuclear energy is the only significant non-fossil source for base load generation. Thus, in a world wanting to limit global warming to within 1.5 or 2 degrees celsius, nuclear energy will have to play a significant role. The share of nuclear energy in India has not gone up as expected. Constraints regarding technology and uranium have been overcome. We now need to address the challenges of financial resources and fast implementation. I do believe that we should attempt to reach as close as possible to the target of 63 GWe by the year 2032. With this, the share of nuclear energy could rise to around 10 per cent of total installed capacity. Although a lot of time has been lost, given that the currently operating capacity and approved projects total up to around 22.5 GWe, an additional 40 GWe capacity needs to be built in the next ten to fifteen years. France and China have completed around forty-five and thirty-five reactors respectively in a span of ten years. Thus, we have a fighting chance to realize our goals if we get our act together.

The current Indian nuclear programme has two streams. The domestic programme and the programme based on international

[17]Solar and wind energy are clean energy sources but are variable in nature. Stabilizing grid when proportion of variable sources becomes large, involves a large investment for storage and control. Nuclear is a clean energy source that is stable and provides for base load generation. This enables an optimum cost even with elimination of fossil energy sources in the grid.

cooperation. Presently, there are hurdles in implementation of the programme under international cooperation. Pricing, it seems, is a major issue. Resorting to competitive bidding for a new standalone project could be a way to discover prices. Maximizing domestic value addition, even for imported projects, is also a way to bring costs down over a period of time. This could also facilitate shifting of the manufacturing base for foreign vendors like Westinghouse to India. A suitable atmosphere will have to be created for foreign companies to set up manufacturing, tie-ups, joint ventures and engagement with local vendors in India. Both NPCIL and DAE have to take initiatives in this context. A lead has to be taken with an eye on the export market. This should be a fallout of the domestic programme.

CREATING AN EXPORT FOOTPRINT

On the nuclear front, India can offer so much to the rest of the world. We have a robust PHWR programme, fast reactors are on the horizon, and soon the thorium reactor will be a reality. With the large programme that is being envisaged, it is important that India becomes a manufacturing hub for nuclear equipment not only for meeting domestic needs, but also for exports. This would help our manufacturing to become competitive. Nuclear trade should thus become a two-way traffic. Our entering the export market in a big way would not only benefit our economy, but also enhance our global standing. Nuclear export is an area we have not paid enough attention to. Countries like China and Argentina managed a better entry in the export market even as they were developing their technology. We do have specific strengths in the context of exports. Our 220 MW PHWR, which has been established as a robust reactor system and which has established global benchmarks of high performance, is the world's smallest commercially competitive system. The system is ideal for emerging economies that have smaller grids. Such a reactor with thorium-low enriched uranium (Th-LEU) fuel becomes even more attractive in the context of increasing global energy needs, and addresses climate change concerns. Th-LEU fuel would enable high burn up, reducing the resultant spent fuel by a factor of eight. The fuel cycle is highly proliferation-resistant and there are added safety advantages. If India can sell such reactors abroad, then we can obtain a double advantage. We can create an export footprint for our nuclear technology and also contribute to addressing a major global challenge—that of climate change. Similarly, going forward, we should look at developing an export version of the Th-LEU-based AHWR, for which the design is ready and is almost immune to any adverse consequences in the public domain, even in case of a rare severe accident.

In an address to scientists and engineers at BARC immediately after the opening up of international civil nuclear cooperation, I had stressed on the importance of the philosophy of self-reliance now more than ever before. Leveraging technology cooperation to enhance our self-reliance and thus do things at even higher levels should be our new strategy. We cannot afford to be dependent on external sources, as such vulnerabilities can be crippling. Self-reliance, however, does not mean building an iron curtain around us, ignoring the technologies available in the open market. We should certainly take advantage of all that is available, but from a position of strength. If we buy from the open market, then we should also be in a position to sell our products and tilt the balance of payments in our favour. A nation cannot grow strong if it does not develop high technology that it is able to market globally. Earlier, self-reliance was a forced choice. Now, in spite of the options available, by choice we should pursue self-reliance so that we remain competitive. Bhabha had actually propounded such self-reliance, even though there were not many restrictions during his time.

The other thing that we need to constantly keep in our minds is the potential vulnerabilities in international civil nuclear cooperation itself. Although a set of multilayered safeguards have been built-in, the real insurance lies in our comparative technological and economic strength. As far as nuclear technology is concerned, the onus in this regard lies with the DAE community. Even if it began through external cooperation, we need to be able to realize complete capability in all aspects of the nuclear programme and take it forward on our own, without external dependence if the need arises. In any case, since we do not subscribe to an once-through fuel cycle[18], we need to extend the programme to second and even third stage through nuclear fuel recycling, which would be based on domestic technology. The developments in the back-end of the nuclear fuel cycle, apart from benefits in terms of additional energy through recycling, are also likely to largely address the problem of disposal of long-lived waste. Through transmutation of almost all nuclear materials and utilization of highly radioactive species like caesium and strontium as radiation or heat sources, it should soon be possible to reduce radio-toxicity of waste arising from nuclear reactors to manageable levels with a relatively shorter radioactive half-life, grossly reducing the demands on a long-term waste repository.

BEYOND ENERGY

I was fortunate to also be associated with other energy domains such as solar energy and the hydrocarbon sector. Even in these

[18]In an open fuel cycle, the spent fuel from nuclear reactors is considered as waste, requiring retrievable disposal in repositories. This has remained an unresolved issue. India does not subscribe to open fuel cycle.

domains there are several challenges that need to be addressed. The large-scale use of solar thermal for 24x7 electricity production as well as for other pyro processes, production of non-fossil hydrogen, large-scale use of biomass to offset a significant fraction of imports, use of coal to produce gas and oil, exploitation of gas hydrates, etc. are some of the priority areas of interest. If we make progress in these areas, it will make a significant difference to the energy security of the country, reduce the import burden and contribute to mitigating the threat of climate change.

Looking beyond energy, I had the privilege of leading the TIFAC program, particularly the preparation of Technology Vision 2035 (TV 2035) for the country. The earlier Technology Vision 2020 was prepared by Dr Abdul Kalam himself. It was decided to look beyond this, with a degree of overlap. We also decided that this exercise should be people-centric, both in terms of its focus as well as its preparation. This massive exercise involved participation of around 5,000 people, representing a diverse set of stakeholders in society. Creating the Technology Vision 2035 for India has been a satisfying experience for me. I am happy that the document captured the attention of many key people in government, both at the centre and in the states, and led to follow-up actions. This work is still in progress.

Finally, I believe that in a society and economy that is well-nurtured with the right education, a deeper and sustained engagement with knowledge would lead to a fundamental transformation. This in turn will lead to the joy of new creation and value. The transactional mindset that normally prevails in a society where knowledge has little role to play in economic activity should evolve into entrepreneurship through deeper engagement with knowledge. The consequent joy of new creation should transform societies towards higher values and wisdom. This is happening in several small pockets. The need of the hour is to make it happen in the larger part of our society and economy—not only in the urban domain, but (perhaps more importantly) in rural India as well.

CHAPTER 13

Celebrating Five Decades of Togetherness

Suyasha Kakodkar

I spent my childhood in different towns in Madhya Pradesh. My father, Dr Ramchandra B. Rishi, was a veterinary doctor and would be transferred often by the government in the course of his work. One such transfer was to the town of Khargone. All Marathi-speaking families living there (around two hundred of them), knew each other well. It was here that we met Kamalatai Kakodkar. My early schooling started in Bal Shiksha Niketan, Kamalatai's Montessori school. I still remember the school and the delicious sweet sheera that we used to get there. I used to participate in singing and dancing events in the annual programme at school. My elder sister and I used to visit her home to study. Though we were familiar with the house, I have no recollection of Anil Kakodkar from that time.

My excellent Montessori education enabled me to get directly enrolled in second grade in the primary school. Later, we moved to Barwani (a town in Madhya Pradesh), while the Kakodkar family moved to Mumbai.

Coincidently, we made frequent visits to Mumbai during our summer vacations, since my maternal uncle stayed at Dadar, in the heart of Mumbai. At times during these vacations, we visited the Kakodkars at their Worli residence. At that time, I could not have imagined that this acquaintance would later lead to my becoming an integral part of the family. My father knew the family well and so the marriage alliance was readily accepted. Till then, we had never met each other personally. My father was well aware of Kakodkar's intelligence, talent and independent nature and was very happy with the alliance.

After marriage, I came to stay at our Worli home. Aai (Kamalatai) always believed that everyone should be gainfully employed and felt that a teacher's job was well-suited for women. So I took admission in a Bachelor of Education (B.Ed.) course, even though I had done a Bachelor of Science (BSc) earlier. Sushama, my sister-in-law, was twelve years old at the time and was studying in school. After the B.Ed. exam, our first daughter, Pallavi, was born in 1971. A few months later, I joined as a teacher at a high school with Bombay Municipal Corporation (BMC). Our younger daughter, Uma, was born in 1973.

Within a year, in 1974, the first peaceful nuclear test experiment took place at Pokhran. Kakodkar was deeply involved in the programme, but as a family, we were blissfully unaware and had a normal family life. Managing a job while raising two small daughters had kept me very busy and I was not aware of the exact nature of his job. I knew that frequent travel was a part of his job, but after the nuclear test, I began to realize the importance of his work. He always downplayed his work or his role to friends and family who enquired about them.

We soon moved to Dhawalgiri, a residential tower in Anushaktinagar, the DAE township at Trombay. BARC was close by, all the facilities were readily available in the colony, and our daughters attended school there. Everything became very convenient. I used to leave early in the morning for school after cooking lunch, and Kakodkar used to get our daughters ready and drop them off at their school next door. Later, as they grew up, they could manage for themselves. Sushama successfully completed her MBBS, after which we got her married. That was the first time after our marriage that we took some family pictures.

Even though we had been staying close to BARC, I couldn't visit the BARC campus for a long time. Neither could our daughters, as at that time only persons above the age of eighteen years were normally allowed entry into the campus. The occasion finally arose when Pallavi won a prize in a Hindi Essay competition and the prize distribution function was organized in the auditorium inside BARC. The Dhruva research reactor project was in progress at that time. This gave us a better appreciation of the new research reactor construction and its complexity. We got a chance to see the work in progress and managed to get some understanding of the scope of Kakodkar's work. I realized the reasons for the increase in his workload and his spending more time in office. As a high school science teacher, this was a great opportunity to educate myself. Kakodkar went to great lengths to answer all our questions.

We rarely went for family vacations. Several Leave Travel Concessions (LTCs), a facility accorded to government employees, lapsed unavailed. In 1983, however, we availed an LTC and visited Goa. I distinctly remember this trip, as it was the first time that we had travelled by an aeroplane. At that time, we did not own a camera and so we do not have any photos of the trip. Kakodkar did not believe in capturing the memories on print; instead he wanted to experience and live in the present. Later we also went to Bangalore with a family friend who was an avid photographer. So we finally got some pictures of one of our rare family vacations.

In December of 2004, we had planned a family vacation to Kerala. We were all travelling by train to Ernakulam and everyone was in a holiday mood. On the way, Kakodkar received a phone call, and the conversation lasted for a long time. I was used to him receiving such calls, but this one was different. When I enquired about it, he told me that it was from Dr Baldev Raj, Director of the IGCAR. A tsunami had devastated the coastline and seawater had entered the DAE residential colony at Kalpakkam near the Madras Atomic Power Plant. The colony was under deluge, with many fatalities. The situation was serious, though the nuclear reactors were safe. The President of India, Dr Abdul Kalam, called and enquired about the situation. Soon after, Mr J.N. Dixit, the then NSA, also called and pledged his support to deal with the situation. Once we reached Ernakulam, Kakodkar informed us that he would be leaving for Kalpakkam immediately. As there were no flights, he had to catch the next available train in an hour's time. Till that time, we had never heard of tsunamis, so we did not realize the havoc it had caused. Losing no time, Kakodkar arrived at Kalpakkam to review the situation and the relief actions. Emotionally connecting with the affected people, creating confidence in them to deal with the grave situation at hand, and strengthening local leadership required a fair amount of time. He was in constant touch with the PMO in Delhi and the DAE office in Mumbai to ensure that all necessary approvals were in place, and relief, restoration and rehabilitation work was launched swiftly. The public also had to be assured that the reactors were safe and there was no radiation-related danger. He joined us again after a few days, once the situation at Kalpakkam was under control.

I used to hear about his promotions, but I never knew the

details of his work. Later, as our daughters grew up and I had extra time, I became more aware of it. As he started becoming a member of different selection committees, including the Chairman of the Atomic Energy Education Society (AEES), my interaction with others who worked with him increased. He would often be invited as a chief guest to many functions and at times I was also invited along with him. This was a new experience for me. I felt privileged to be able to attend some of these functions and got a ringside view of the side conversations, which were mostly related to reactor engineering. One could see the passion and conviction he had towards his work. Often people used to come to our home in the evenings and weekends to have extended discussions that could not be held at the workplace. These discussions would go on for long hours.

When he became the Head of the Reactor Engineering Division (RED), I realized that my very identity had started changing. People started recognizing me. We moved to Shantiniketan, another residential building in Anushaktinagar that houses senior officers of the DAE. We delayed moving there till Uma completed her tenth grade, mainly because the school was right next door and that was very convenient. All such decisions were always based on the convenience of the whole family and not on the norms of level or grade in the office.

When MAPS, located at Kalpakkam, developed a critical failure, the responsibility to repair the reactors was entrusted to Kakodkar. The initial plan was for him to visit it for a day and accordingly he had not packed any extra sets of clothes. But the work extended and he had to stay back for one full week. He used to wash and dry his clothes overnight and wear them again the next day. He could have gone out and bought some clothes, but then that would have taken precious time away from his work. Later I also learnt from his colleague that he had spent a continuous forty-eight hours inside the reactor control room at that time. He would always completely immerse himself in his work with unwavering dedication and had a hunger to learn. He never ever complained about any hardships in any of his assignments—personal or professional. In fact, he loved accepting new and challenging assignments and was always confident about delivering on them.

> *'Let me not pray to be sheltered from dangers,*
> *but to be fearless in facing them.*
> *Let me not beg for the stilling of my pain, but*
> *for the heart to conquer it.'*
>
> —RABINDRANATH TAGORE

Once, he had to travel to Lonavala by car for a lecture a day before Ganesh Chaturthi.[19] Hence he brought the Ganesh idol home on the previous day. The next day he left early in the morning. It was raining that day, and they had to travel through the winding western 'ghat' of the Sahyadri mountain range. Their car skidded and toppled over the median to the other side. A little later, Kakodkar and the driver got out of the toppled car with the help of the locals. Luckily, both were unhurt. They contacted the organizers at Lonavala and requested them to send another car. Kakodkar proceeded to deliver the lecture as planned. At home, we were completely unaware of the accident. Later in the day when someone from the office contacted us to check on him, I had no idea and simply said that he was out of town that day for work. We came to know about the details of the accident and the miraculous escape only a day later, as he did not want

[19]Ganesh festival is celebrated as a major social event all over Maharashtra for ten days following Ganesh Chaturthi. We also celebrate the ten-day event in our house, during which we worship Lord Ganesh.

the family to get anxious. Kakodkar believed that since there was no injury, there seemed to be no point in discussing or reliving the incident and wasting precious time. For me, though, it was a shock, followed by relief, that a major calamity had been avoided due to the grace of Lord Ganesh.

Both our daughters did well in their school and later pursued engineering. Both chose their life partners on their own. Kakodkar has always advised and provided his complete perspective to our children for every major decision. But he has let the children make own their decisions, which has helped them to become strong, independent working women. Both the couples spent about eight years in the US in the early parts of their professional careers before returning to India.

In 1996, when Kakodkar became Director, BARC, we shifted to Zerlina, another residential tower at Malabar Hills meant for the highest ranking officers of the department. I got a transfer to a school nearby. I also got promoted to Supervisor. My school timings changed to the general shift, and both of us were busy in our daily schedules.

Kakodkar was awarded the Padma Shri in 1998. I visited Delhi for the first time during the awards ceremony. It gave me an opportunity to see a lot of prominent personalities like President K.R. Narayanan, Prime Minister Atal Bihari Vajpayee, Lal Krishna Advani and George Fernandes up close—dignitaries who, till then, I had only heard of or seen on television. It was a very exciting time. I also got to meet Dr Abdul Kalam personally later in the evening, along with other families of the awardees. I feel truly blessed to have met such eminent personalities.

In May of the same year, the second nuclear test was carried out. I had plans to visit my daughters in the US during my summer vacations in May, but was asked to postpone my trip till the end of the month. I was a little disappointed, as the school had closed for the summers and I preferred spending maximum time with my daughters. I realized the reason for this only later and felt proud that Kakodkar had a higher mission to fulfil. There were many such events that we came to know of only after they had occurred, given their national importance and the need to maintain secrecy around them.

However, after the tests, Anil was worried about the safety of our children in the US due to the nature of his work. This was the period when various international negotiations had begun. We are glad that they have all come back to India and are doing well. Pallavi, her husband Anand, and their sons Ameya and Aneesh live in Hyderabad. Uma, her husband Ramachandran, their daughter Shruti and their son Dhruva live in Bengaluru.

The next year, in 1999, when Kakodkar was awarded the Padma Bhushan, Aai and I went together to attend the function. I felt happy and proud to be present to cheer him, although our children were not around this time either.

In 2000 he was appointed the Chairman of the AEC. He started several new initiatives. His workload and pace of work increased even further. People became aware of the importance of nuclear energy, and BARC as an organization became more visible as a premier institution doing groundbreaking research. At that time, I was posted in a school at Mahim as a Vice Principal, and later became the Principal of Jagannath Shankar Sheth Municipal School at Nana Chowk, a place very close to our residence. As a result, I became more involved in the school administration. We now shifted to a bigger flat in the same building.

There was a steady stream of visitors who came for meetings and discussions. Kakodkar's work pace, schedules and activity kept increasing over the years. Around that time, discussions on international civil nuclear cooperation were ongoing. Nuclear energy was constantly in the news—on TV and in the print media. But the atmosphere at home was, as always, very calm and casual. The daily routine remained the same. He would still come home and adjust the cushions, the sheets, the carpet or one or another table that was not aligned. Kakodkar's perfection can be seen in all spheres of life. Even today, his suitcase is always packed and ready for moving at a short notice. The clothes are always perfectly folded and neatly arranged—even in the middle of the night or in the wee hours of morning. Whatever be the time, things must always be in order for himself—but there is no expectation of anyone else doing the same.

As always, he kept us shielded from the problems at work. We were completely unaware of the pressures on him while negotiating the Indo-US Agreement for Civil Nuclear Cooperation. We came to know of it only afterwards, when he acknowledged it. It was much later, when we read about it in the newspapers, that we understood how he was holding his own against so many powerful people in the interests of the country.

He received several accolades later for his contribution to bringing India into the nuclear mainstream and thereby enhancing India's stature. He was awarded the Padma Vibhushan in 2009. By this time, both our daughters had returned to India. So, all of us, including our daughters Pallavi and Uma and our sister Sushama, could attend the ceremony. This was a memorable occasion for our family.

In September 2009, IAEA organized its annual General Conference at Vienna. The AEC team, with Kakodkar, participated in it as always. I also got a chance to visit Vienna. I had not been able to travel much with him earlier due to my work or family commitments. Representatives from many member states of IAEA attended this conference and delivered their statements. Kakodkar was also to deliver an address there, so I expressed my interest in attending it. I was told that usually, such requests are not honoured. But the local organizers contacted the IAEA office and I was allowed to attend his address. They had made special provisions to allow me to attend. I felt privileged to be able to hear his address in person, along with all the international delegates.

Every two years, Bruhan Maharashtra Mandal of North America organizes a conference in the USA. In the year 2011, we were invited as chief guests for the conference in Chicago. This organization has around 4,000 Marathi-speaking members from all over the USA. It felt nice to see so many Marathi families gathered together at Chicago for the event. We also visited Fermilab at Batavia, Illinois, during this trip. It felt amazing to explore this huge research complex. Furthermore, we visited the Stanford and Berkeley Universities in California and met a few Indian students there. It gave me perspective on the magnitude of research activities happening in these world-class universities.

Apart from the national awards, I am very proud that he has also been awarded the highest state awards by all three states we have been connected with—the Gomant Vibhushan award by the state of Goa in 2010, the Maharashtra Bhushan award by the government of Maharashtra in 2011–12 and the Madhya Pradesh Gaurav award by the government of Madhya Pradesh in 2014. Kakodkar has received a steady stream of awards and accolades over the years.

After his retirement in the year 2009, we are now settled in Thane, adjacent to Mumbai. In the initial time after retirement, I thought that Kakodkar's work hours would finally be reduced. He fell sick within a year after retiring and was admitted to a hospital. At the time, his medical file in the BARC hospital was practically empty, as he had rarely visited the hospital as a patient during the forty-five years of his service. After he recovered, he got engaged in much broader areas of interest, well beyond nuclear energy.

He is passionate about spreading awareness of science and technology in society. He realized that there is a basic gap in the younger recruits because of a lack of exposure to the industry. It is his belief that promoting hands-on learning and applied technology and research for every student is the need of the hour. To this end, he has helped shape the Technology Vision for 2035, which had previously been drafted by Dr Abdul Kalam as Technology Vision 2020. As a Chairman of RGSTC and a part of several other organizations that he is connected with, as either Chairman or a member on their apex bodies, he continues to guide and mentor activities related to science-led societal development.

He still travels extensively and continues to be engrossed in his work. The pace and rate of his engagements continue unabated, with an average of three days a week spent travelling. Kakodkar has become more relaxed now that he plays the role of a mentor, guide and advisor. But his connection with students and the community at large has increased over the years, and he uses his network to help entrepreneurs, students and professionals. He enjoys learning and promoting technology for progress, and presently devotes his time primarily to issues of energy, education and science-based development.

In the last fifty years of our married life, Anil has time and again exhibited the qualities of being self-reliant, modest, determined, dedicated, objective and scientific. Above all, pursuit towards excellence has been undeterred. He has dedicated his life to the nation, following the footsteps of his Gandhian, freedom-fighter parents. At the same time, he is the binding force of our family. I am fortunate and blessed to have such a life partner, who is a perfectionist with high integrity.

I am often reminded of these lines from the famous poet Robert Frost's poem 'Stopping by Woods on a Snowy Evening'. They very aptly describe his zeal for work even today:

The woods are lovely, dark, and deep.
But I have promises to keep,
And miles to go before I sleep,
And miles to go before I sleep.

CHAPTER 14

Dada, My Doting Brother

Janhavi Gangal

I distinctly remember the night of 25 December 1997. My Aai,[20] my Dada Anil Kakodkar, and I were in Delhi. We usually travel with our boisterous, large families. But this time, it was just the three of us. We were meeting our ailing father, who was undergoing treatment for chronic myeloid leukaemia (CML) at Ram Manohar Lohia Hospital. The problem had relapsed and his condition was serious. That was the first time I had ever met him. We tried to persuade him to come along with us to Mumbai, but in vain. Disheartened, we returned to our guest house. Tired after the travel and a hectic day at the hospital, Aai and I turned in for the night. But Dada excused himself and began working at a study desk, almost certainly on a topic of national importance.

The scene felt very familiar and brought back memories from four decades ago. My world was very small then, with just the three of us—Aai, Dada and I, living in our small home at Adarsh Nagar in Prabhadevi, Bombay. Aai would work all day and pull the family together and Dada would study diligently at his desk

[20]As we lovingly address our mother in Marathi

late through the night, taking the family ahead.

Alongside the struggle for India's Independence, our father was also deeply involved in the Goa Independence Movement and was arrested and deported to Portugal in 1946, for nine years. As a result, Aai nurtured Dada single-handedly in Khargone, a small town in Madhya Pradesh. There he studied up to matriculation. Finally, in 1956, our father was released from Lisbon, and Aai and Dada shifted to Mumbai, looking to live as a family while Dada pursued his education to become an engineer. However, Goa was yet to be liberated and fate had a different trick up its sleeve for us. Soon after my birth in 1957, my father decided to go back to work for the Goa independence struggle. He became active in politics and relieved himself of family bonds and responsibilities for Dada's education, my upbringing, etc. That put Aai under tremendous strain—mentally, physically and financially. Her health deteriorated—yet she had to work till Dada's education was complete.

When Dada joined Ruparel College, our daily routine would start when Dada would leave for college early in the morning. Aai would carry me by bus to a day care in Dadar, and then go to office in Erla near Cooper Hospital, Andheri—a total distance of 12 km. Dada would take me home from the day care after college and look after me until Aai returned. He didn't have the luxury of indulging in extracurricular college activities like other boys of his age. After a long day at work, Aai would come home and start cooking meals, and engage with both of us. She was always keen to enquire about everything that happened in our day, over dinner, in a very jovial atmosphere. I was oblivious to the problems that the family was facing. Only after I slept did Dada and Aai discuss their financial and other problems. Dada would then study late into the night at his desk. But decades before worrying about the responsibility of DAE and its seventeen-odd establishments, this young seventeen-year-old had much to worry about—his mother's health, his sister's education, and a precarious financial situation in the exorbitant city of Bombay that would force his mother to continue working for another few years, until he could start earning.

Our neighbours in the colony were textile mill workers. They would return late in the night after their shift and were very appreciative of Dada's work ethic. However, this often made other kids envious of Dada, and they in turn would be very nasty to him. I can only imagine how difficult this must have been for a teenager who was far ahead of his age in terms of maturity and capability.

The early '60s were particularly tough on Aai. She struggled against all odds with meagre finances and the spectre of ill health weighing her down. Having to show up for work through her illness left her with no time for a full recovery. Dada was our only hope to break out of this vicious spiral. He was well aware of the quandary. He had a single-minded focus on graduating as an engineer at the earliest, being independent, and starting to earn so that she could rest. In spite of meagre means and the daily struggle of making ends meet, Aai planted in us an implicit but uncompromising emphasis on patriotism, self-reliance, knowledge, hardwork and dedication. It would take another three decades for the seeds sown at that time to bear fruit.

After graduating from VJTI, he joined the prestigious BARC and forced Aai to retire and rest at home to recover from illness. As a result, her health finally improved. Moreover, I got her complete attention during my formative years. But his work didn't, however, detract in any way from the deep love and care that he had for us.

During my school days, I used to take my doubts about science concepts and maths problems to him. He never gave me direct answers or spoon-fed me. He would encourage me to read the text thoroughly and understand it step by step. If I still had queries, he would explain the concept by giving different examples and puzzles. In the process, my queries would be answered and the concepts clearly understood.

He encouraged me in school and in college while I was choosing my career. So is the case with both his daughters. However busy he is, he always has the time for us. We can all discuss our problems and clear any doubts we have about any decision we have to take. He listens patiently, understands our anxiety, and discusses various aspects and ideas—the whole thought process. He will never preach, nor instruct directly, but will help us in taking the decision.

Regardless of any other pressing issues, he was and still is always available and present for the family in times of need. I was only ten years old when riots broke out in Bombay in 1967. Dada was abroad in Nottingham for his postgraduate studies in Structural Engineering. Rioters broke into and looted Worli's Century Bazar; buses were set ablaze and the government milk booth and the cooperative fish stall fell victim to the rioters. From the window of our house, less than a hundred feet away, we saw them throw burning logs through wooden slots. To make matters worse, the fish stalls had industry-grade cold storages with large gas compressors. It was literally a high-pressure situation.

As the army arrived and curfew was imposed later in the evening, we thought the crowd had dispersed. However, they had merely taken shelter under the staircase of our building. They were urgently seeking a temporary shelter and started threatening us. Aai and I were alone and scared of the rioters now gathered at the gate. We sorely missed Dada's comforting presence. At about 9 PM, the cold storage suddenly burst with a terrifying blast, and the whole fish stall caught fire and spewed burning splinters all around. Massive wood and metal pieces crashed on our window. We could not withstand the heat even from inside the house. Burning pieces of wood were showering down on the house like fireballs and we had to struggle till midnight to close all the windows and save our house from catching fire.

Sometime after midnight, after the fish-booth had been reduced to ashes, we decided to retire to bed, when the doorbell rang. Scared that the rioters were still lurking, we asked who it was. 'Postman', he whispered in a stressful, hurried voice. 'I have a telegraph for you from UK.' It was a reply paid telegraph from Dada, after watching news reports of riots around our house on the BBC. The communication technology back in those days made it especially challenging to instantly reach out like this. Through the embers, Dada had reached out in our hours of fear. That moment we felt his warm presence so near to us that the fear of facing such a difficult situation alone vanished in no time.

Following these riots and Aai's short illness, Dada decided to return immediately after his MS exams and thesis submission without spending a single extra day abroad. Sightseeing or spending time relishing the last moments of student life never mattered to him. The people in our neighbourhood would often say that he would never come back, or even if he did, he would be a changed person. But he returned just the same—my loving and caring Dada.

His behaviour at home and with others never changed even after the meteoric rise in his career. We would often learn about his promotions and achievements only from his colleagues, and about special tasks like the nuclear tests at Pokhran from the newspapers. He has travelled all over the world, but never glamourized it, nor compared or criticized the conditions in our country. He would instead describe novel things and remarkable, useful innovations that he had observed during his travels.

I remember he had sent me the literature and newspaper reporting on 'Apollo's first landing on the moon', which got me interested in science.

I have always felt his support throughout my life. I remember the day I was to appear for my National Talent Search (NTS) exam at Churchgate, Mumbai. A nationwide strike was declared that day and we expected large-scale disruption of public transport. I seriously contemplated not going for the exam, but the importance he laid on academics was far above such local disruptions. The goal was a lot more important and buses were just one way to get to the examination centre—one could always walk. I didn't quite appreciate how seriously he meant it at that time but I found out the next morning. We reached the college early in the morning by train, but later all public transport was halted. I was oblivious of it but Dada and a cousin walked back home to Prabhadevi for lunch and back again to Churchgate to pick me up in the evening, and the three of us again walked back home. Churchgate to Prabhadevi—a distance of about 10 km—thrice in a day is a trivial journey when one has the right perspective.

He has influenced all of us. He is simple and humble, but confident. He is a man of few words, and makes precise and assertive (not argumentative) statements. Most importantly, he influences others by his commitment to his work, his mission, and his duty.

On 2 May 1998, we lost our father. This was just a few days prior to the successive nuclear tests at Pokhran—of which no one had a clue. Dada was intensely busy with the highly technical, intricate preparations under the highest level of secrecy and security. To maintain the secrecy without raising any suspicions, he decided to go to Delhi for the last rites all alone. Unaware of his plans, we expressed our wish to accompany him. He declined.

That was uncharacteristic of him. However, we insisted that at least my husband, Dr Ravi Gangal, accompany him, to which he finally agreed. He performed the last rites, simultaneously monitoring the developments at Pokhran secretly. He neither showed his emotions nor the tensions of the challenging mission ahead. Even my husband did not have the slightest inkling of what was going on in his mind. After the last rites, he immediately rushed away for 'urgent work'—which the whole world came to know about a few days later. He performed his duties both as a son and as a son of the nation.

The one who is calm, steady, undisturbed and focused on work even during testing times reflects the true essence of a Karmayogi, or a man devoted to work. He accepted all the recognition and rewards conferred on him, including the Padma Awards (three of the highest civilian awards bestowed by the Government of India), with great humility and never rested on his laurels. Greater responsibility brought in him a greater focus to align the numerous organizations under the DAE umbrella and a greater drive to reshape them, following the profound vision of its founding father, Dr Homi Bhabha. Challenges and opportunities like the nuclear tests at Pokhran to the now-famous 123 Agreement (Indo–US Agreement for Civil Nuclear Cooperation) were handled with intelligence, equanimity and principled resolve to further our country's energy independence.

Now, after his retirement, he continues to devote his time to issues related to energy, education, and science-based societal development. Being associated with many eminent institutes of national importance, he travels far and wide. Naturally, all of us at home are concerned about his health. But for my Dada, work is worship.

CHAPTER 15

Ekalavya—My Friend, Philosopher and Guide

Suresh Gangotra

After working in BARC for about twenty-five years, I joined the DAE Secretariat in May 2009 as part of the Strategic Planning Group. One day, I received communication from the Chairman's office to prepare a one-page draft of a message that was to be printed in the souvenir of an organization related to quizzing on metallurgy. I sent the hard copy of the draft by 6:00 PM. The next day, at about 10:30 AM, the draft was returned with a note, 'Fair up', neatly written by hand with a pencil and initialled 'AK'. I wondered when Dr Kakodkar had read and approved the draft. When I enquired with a colleague, he said, 'Don't you know about the suitcases?' He told me about two suitcases that would go to the residence of Dr Kakodkar in the evening, full of papers and files, and would be returned the next morning. During my sittings with Dr Kakodkar, one day I asked him to expand on the mystery of the suitcases. I am glad I did, because I got an insight into his working style. In his own words:

'Let me start at the beginning. I have evolved my own style of working, my governance, if I can say so myself. When I became Group Director in BARC, I was given a room with an annex for my Personal Assistant (PA). It was the first time that I had a PA. Because of the post and the office setup, there was a tendency for a gap to be created between the senior and the juniors. Anyone wanting to see the superior had to come through his PA, seek his permission, and meet him only after. The way to the senior's chamber was through the PA's room. I felt that this was unfair. I unlocked the door that opened to the common corridor, and pasted a sign saying "DISTURB" on the door. I told my PA that scientists and engineers were the most important stakeholders, and they should have easy access to me, even if it was for personal problems. Some colleagues advised me that for efficient management, I should maintain distance from juniors. The juniors should not be allowed to take liberties with me. I replied that I was well aware of that, but juniors should refrain from taking such liberties out of respect, not fear. They also said that if I allowed free access, then I would be disturbed all the time and not be able to do my work. I said that if there was so much tension in the system, then it was better that I be disturbed. For me, people have always been the number one priority. For a moment I wondered whether I was doing the right thing, because I was slightly apprehensive about being disturbed in my work. Nevertheless, I decided to go ahead. To be fair to my juniors and colleagues, in the four years that I held that office, it was only twice that someone came to meet me directly. That too, after 6:00 PM—well beyond office closing time. In spite of my door being kept open, almost everyone approached me through the PA and with my permission.

'The different divisions of BARC were co-located in an engineering hall. The shop floors were full of equipment set up for experiments. I was part of the housekeeping team and was a stickler for cleanliness. I would take frequent rounds of the shop floors. If I noticed stray equipment lying unused or unattended, I would get stickers pasted on the equipment

for the user to remove to its proper place. In case it was not done, the unclaimed equipment would be removed by the housekeeping team. I did not like passages being blocked or junk strewn around.

'When I was appointed Director, BARC, Joseph, the Administrative Officer, came to see me in my office. I wanted to carry forward the same culture to the Director's Office. I was requested not to do so because the Director had many visitors, often foreigners. It would not be proper to be disturbed by all and sundry. I was, however, assured that nobody would be denied access to me. As Director, I started an open forum where the staff could meet the Director and raise any issues. I sustained it for a few sittings, but soon realized that it had been reduced to a very small number of habitual complainers, who raised issues just for the sake of attracting attention. I had to close it soon.

'There were serious challenges when I moved to OYC as Chairman. Even as the performance of nuclear power plants was improving, supplies of uranium, the fuel for the reactors, was dwindling. There was fear of NPCIL going in red in the absence of adequate fuel supply. NFC, the fuel manufacturer, could face worker unrest due to reduced production. UCIL was at the receiving end, as it was responsible for supplying uranium. I looked at the problem comprehensively and created a discussion platform. Each organization connected with fuel was included and weekly meetings were held where outstation members would join in on video conference. Everybody started looking at the problem collectively and began finding solutions. [As mentioned earlier, A.B. Awati], a geologist working in DAE, suggested tapping the Tummalapalle mine for uranium. The idea came out of this forum. The synergy in the group helped tide over the problem. In a similar manner, an open forum for senior officers at DAE was created. I would meet them every week, without an agenda and without any record of discussions. All officers above the rank of Joint Secretary and equivalent would be invited.

'The story about the suitcases: When I was Group Director, I found time in office to look at paperwork. After I became Director, BARC, the

paperwork increased. And in OYC, it was even more. From BARC, I used to carry papers home. It would be one suitcase-load. And after going to OYC, the suitcases became two. I never looked at papers in office unless they were absolutely essential. The whole day would be spent holding meetings or seeing people. People took priority over paperwork. I would go through the files and papers at my residence. After I had met the last person seeking appointment with me in office, I would go home. After some relaxation, I would have my dinner and when everyone went to sleep, I would get on with the suitcases. At the Chairman's residence in South Mumbai, where I was staying, there is an office for him to work in. It would begin around 11:00 PM and take me two to four hours to go through all the papers. Occasionally, it would be 4:00 AM in the morning when I finished. I would then go to sleep, get up by 7:00 AM and be in office by 8:30 AM. I had instructed my staff in office that no paper should remain in my office for more than thirty-six hours. As a result, the more I cleared, the more papers started coming to my office. But people would always take priority. On my desk at BARC, I had a quote, "If you kill someone's idea, you kill a little bit of that person." I have always believed in this maxim. It has great merit and has helped me often.

'I specially recollect my interaction with V.P. Raja, the then Joint Secretary in DAE. Raja was an able administrator and well-read. He had a degree in Physics and had been reading extensively about nuclear energy on the Internet. Unfortunately, there is a lot of negative information there, and that would be reflected in our discussions on issues. However, after a few discussions of mutual engagement, we were on the same page. Over time, he became a champion of nuclear energy—so much so that he started public awareness programmes in his I&M section. On his own initiative, he published booklets extolling the benefits of atomic energy in many Indian languages. He and his initiatives in addressing issues became assets to the Department.'

When I asked Dr Kakodkar about his hobbies, he had this to say:

'During my childhood days in Khargone, we used to have Ganpati mela, a kind of religious fair. There used to be group singing of hymns in praise of Lord Ganesha. I used to take active part and was the lead singer. My mother noticed my aptitude for singing and appointed a music tutor to train me. Soon she noticed that the singing was affecting my studies and promptly stopped my music classes. That was the end of my musical journey. When I came to Bombay, I enrolled in the swimming pool and would regularly go for swimming. After I moved to Anushaktinagar, the residential colony near BARC, I thought of learning tennis. After a few promotions in office, my assignments grew. I began staying late in office and there was no time left for tennis or any other hobby.

'There was another attempt by me to utilize my spare time fruitfully. I had done a course in project management from the National Institute of Industrial Engineering. I wanted to have a formal degree in management. Accordingly, I secured admission for part-time management study at the Jamnalal Bajaj Institute of Management Studies in Bombay. After I paid the fees, I thought of seeking permission from BARC, though it was not mandatory. On seeing my application, Dr Ramanna, the Director, called me. He dissuaded me from studying management, saying that it was a waste of time. Instead, I could spend my free time playing tennis in Anushaktinagar. I sensed that he was apprehensive that after I obtained a degree in management, I would quit. I assured him that if that was what he thought, then he was wrong. I genuinely wanted to study management. In any case, if I wanted to quit, I did not have to wait for any degree in management. I was confident of acquiring a decent job at any time. Finally, I told him that I would respect any decision that he took on my application. But I also asked him to promise that BARC should not stop any employee in the future who wanted to pursue any course. It would only improve their skills. If BARC could allow scientists to pursue PhD, then what was the objection to other

courses? To my surprise, he agreed to my suggestion, but did not allow me to study management. I had to forfeit my fees.'

I asked him whether he had taken an IQ test. This is what he said:

'I have not taken an IQ test, but I am sure that if I take one the score will be just average. I would like to tell you about this incident in BARC. Dr Ramanna was the Director, and he had identified a group of twenty-five scientists and engineers to be exposed to a month-long management course conducted by a Professor from IIM, Bangalore. The course included lectures, group discussions, group activities and home assignments. At the end of the course, the Professor gave feedback on each one of us, based on his interactions with us. Normally, experts tend to bracket people into different types as per their estimation, but in my case the professor said that he was unable to judge me. He found me complex.'

I hinted that this could be a sign of genius. Dr Kakodkar strongly disagreed. *'Except for a few prodigies, nobody is a genius. You are not born intelligent, you become one because of your environment. Every person is shaped by his environment. If at all I have become something, I attribute it to my upbringing, to my environment—to which I am utterly grateful. You become a genius if you are passionate and committed to what you do.'*

We were picking photographs to be included in this book. There is a picture of his childhood (see photos) where one can't miss his piercing gaze. I remarked that even today he has intense concentration. I commented on his stamina and focus. I have myself noticed, as have many others who have interacted with him, that when you see him in the morning, he is always well groomed with hair set perfectly. He would sit through a meeting till almost 8:00 PM at night, but his appearance would not change—not a single strand of hair would be out of place. He laughed and replied that he never felt the need for any breaks when he was busy working. He could carry on for long hours because he enjoyed his work.

Since he joined BARC in 1963 and Dr Homi Bhabha died in 1966, I asked him if he had any note from Dr Bhabha that could be included in the book. He said, *'You have struck a nerve. As a topper from the BARC training school, I was presented with a book on mechanical engineering. It was personally signed by Dr Bhabha, congratulating me on my achievement. Alas! I have misplaced it. Though I have a personal collection of about a thousand books, this one has not been found for the last thirty years. Books have a strange way of walking away. It is possible that someone borrowed it and forgot to return it.'* I responded that it would be a collector's delight, and was definitely a great loss. To that, his reply was philosophical: *'There are many things in life that we lose. But we should live in the present and life must go on.'*

On an impulse, one day I asked him whether he is an introvert. *'Yes, very much'* was the reply. *'Not only an introvert, I am a loner. When I was a student, my colleagues would invite me to group studies. I would always reject them and never joined anyone for studying.'* I found a contradiction in this statement. I reminded him that in office, the whole day he would be talking to people, either on phone or in person or in meetings. Was that not a trait of an extrovert? He replied, *'I talked in office because that was my job. But I am an introvert. Maybe it has something to do with my childhood.'*

I was left speechless, gazing at this emotional gentleman—the epitome of humility, genius, diligence, and honesty, and a nationalist to the core.

Acknowledgements

We have no words to express our gratitude to Dr Manmohan Singh for his foreword to this book. His support and understanding of atomic energy and its self-reliant development have been a source of strength for us. Dr CNR Rao, Shri MK Narayanan, Dr ElBaradei, Dr Bigot, Dr Kasturirangan, Shri Tarun Das and Shri Swapnesh Malhotra have written very gracious endorsements. We are overwhelmed by their words, which will remain treasures for us.

This book is the result of the hard work and inputs of many people who have helped us. We are grateful to them. Swapnesh Malhotra has also provided the explanation of India's three-stage nuclear programme in a manner that is easy to understand. Ravi Shankar and Manhar Patel have contributed by providing some of the photographs and even enhancing them, since they belong to times long before the advent of digital photography. Given the technical nature of the narrative, C.S. Viswanadham, Dr Namera Neena Bopaiah and Latha Nair have meticulously gone through the text to check for errors and suggest corrections. This has helped in making the text understandable for a reader who is new to the subject. Vishal Jadi has been helpful in facilitating numerous meetings and discussions. We are also grateful to team Rupa for their work on the book.

Index

Institute of Chemical Technology (ICT), 128, 152

International Thermonuclear Experimental Reactor (ITER), 95-96, 120